VICTIMS OF SOCIAL INJUSTICE
A Study of
Women Landless Labourers

About the Authors

Prof. Hajira Kumar, Head, Department of Social Work, Jamia Millia Islamia (A Central University), New Delhi has been associated with teaching, research and extension for the last three decades. She is also providing professional and technical assistance to a number of NGOs, Ministries and Departments of Social Work, in other universities. She had been the Honorary Director of Sarojini Naidu Centre for Women Studies, Jamia Millia Islamia for four years. Her contribution in the literature of social-work is note worthy. Besides several articles, she has seven books at her credit such as – Voluntary Action and the Financial Gap (1988), Social Work – An Experience and an Experiment in India (1993), Theories in Social Work Practice (1995), Social Work, Social Development and Sustainable Development (1997), Status of Muslim Women in India (2002), Social Work and Developmental Issues (2005) and Women's Empowerment: Issues, Challenges and Strategies – A Source Book (2005). Muslim women are one of her areas of interest. A book 'Family Planning among the Muslims' is in the press. Her style is simple and interesting. It encourages every reader to develop his own thinking.

Dr. Jaimon Varghese, a social work practitioner and a guest faculty in Department of Social Work, Delhi University has been a keen researcher on the issue of women empowerment. He did his Master in Social Work and M.A. in Psychology. He has also earned PG Diploma in Labour Welfare and PG Diploma in Office Management. His association with an NGO St. Joseph's Service Society is several years old in various capacities. He had been the project officer for four research projects undertaken by Sarojini Naidu Centre for Women Studies (SNCWS), Jamia Millia Islamia. He did his doctoral research on the topic of Empowerment of Women Literacy Workers in 2006. He is co-author of a source book 'Women's Empowerment: Issues, Challenges and Strategies—A Source Book. (2005). Besides, he has several research-based articles on his credit. In other words he blended in him an active grassroots level worker a researcher and a teacher.

VICTIMS OF SOCIAL INJUSTICE
A Study of Women Landless Labourers

Hajira Kumar
Jaimon Varghese

CONCEPT PUBLISHING COMPANY, NEW DELHI-110059

Cataloging in Publication Data—DK
Courtesy: D.K. Agencies (P) Ltd. docinfo@dkagencies.com

Kumar, Hajira, 1948-
Victims of social injustice : a study of women landless labourers / Hajira Kumar, Jaimon Varghese.
p. cm.
Study conducted among the selected labours from the states of Delhi, Uttar Pradesh and Haryana, India.
Includes bibliographical references (p.)
Includes index.
ISBN 13: 9788180694738
ISBN 10: 8180694739

1. Women agricultural laborers—India—Social conditions. 2. Women agricultural laborers—India—Economic conditions. 3. Rural women—Employment—India. 4. Harassment—India. 5. Women agricultural laborers—Government policy—India.
I. Varghese, Jaimon, 1970-, joint author. II. Title.

DDC 305.489 623 095 4 22

This book is based on a study sponsored by the Ministry of Human Resource Development, Government of India and it is published with due permission

Hajira Kumar and **Jaimon Varghese**

ISBN -13: 978-81-8069-473-8
ISBN -10: 81-8069-473-9

First Published 2008

Published and Printed by
Ashok Kumar Mittal
Concept Publishing Company
A/15-16, Commercial Block, Mohan Garden
New Delhi-110059 (India)

Phones : 25351460, 25351794
Fax : 091-11-25357103
Email : publishing@conceptpub.com

Dedicated to

All the marginalised Women
of India

PREFACE

Landless unorganised female labour force is probably the most miserable section of the society. They work on the farms of others during season. Rest of the time, they remain unemployed. Landless labourers, especially women are involved in most precarious and least rewarding work. Despite the fact that these agricultural workers comprises more than 70 million all over India, they are highly marginalised, extremely deprived and excluded from the mainstream society. They are placed at the lowest level of poverty. Wage structure for them is highly discriminatory. Not only this, they often suffer from work place harassment.

Their problems are compounded by the fact that they are neglected in all welfare and developmental programmes meant specifically for women. They are unidentified and "invisible" inspite of being a big group. Also, they cannot get any protection of legal provisions, as they are not a part of organised labour. Due to illiteracy and lack of awareness they have no knowledge of their "welfare rights". It is against this backdrop that the study has attempted to unearth the magnitude and intensity of the problems these women workers are facing. Any endeavour towards intervening for improving their lot requires examining the role of various socio-political institutions and the impact of governmental and non-governmental welfare activities if any, on the studied group. The study has explored new and evolving needs of these women workers in the present scenario. Besides, it has tried to suggest some measures which can bring about some improvement in their life style, mental make up and socio-economic situation. It could be a good reading material for research scholars, social science students and NGO functionaries working in the field.

New Delhi

Hajira Kumar
Jaimon Varghese

ACKNOWLEDGEMENTS

The study is an outcome of collective efforts of the whole research staff of the centre and many other academicians working intensively in the field.

First of all I must express my gratitude to Mr. Qazi Zaheer Hasan who has spent his precious time for editing the text of this report. His patient and keen corrections have significantly improved the quality of the final report.

I wish to express my thanks to the Ministry of Human Resource Development for sponsoring an innovative study and enabling us to provide some suggestions.

I am thankful to all the members of advisory and standing committees for giving their support and cooperation whenever it was required. I am particularly grateful to the special advisors.

I must gratefully remember the hard work done by the research staff and the support provided by the other staff of the centre.

I want to extend my thanks to the Department of Social Work, Jamia Millia Islamia for all kinds of administrative support.

Last but not the least I am highly obliged to all the respondents who have given detailed insights of their private lives for the cause of landless women labourers.

I want to express my gratitude to many others who remain unnoticed but have helped in the process of data collection and report preparation.

I must admit that so many people should get the credit for the hard work, which is reflected, in the study. However, the shortcomings in this study are only due to my limitations.

Hajira Kumar

CONTENT

ABBREVIATIONS

AIDS	Acquired Immune Deficiency Syndrome
BDO	Block Development Officer
BHC	Benzene Hexa Chloride
BPL	Below Poverty Line
BSY	Balika Samriddhi Yojana
CEDAW	Convention on Elimination of Discrimination Against Women
CSW	Commission on the Status of Women
CSWB	Central Social Welfare Board
DAW	Division for the Advancement of Women
DPAP	Drought Prone Area Programme
DWACRA	Development of Women and Child in Rural Areas
DWCD	Department of Women and Child Development
DWCUA	Development of Women and Children in the Urban Areas
ESI	Employees State Insurance
FAL	Female Agricultural Labour
GDP	Gross Domestic Product
GOI	Government of India
HDI	Human Development Index
HIV	Human Immuno-deficiency Virus
HT	Hindustan Times
IFAD	International Fund for Agricultural Development
IGNOU	Indira Gandhi National Open University
IIT	Indian Institute of Technology
ILO	International Labour Organisation
IMR	Infant Mortality Rate

IMY	Indira Mahila Yojana
IPC	Indian Penal Code
IRDP	Integrated Rural Development Programme
JGSY	Jawahar Gram Samridhi Yojana
JMI	Jamia Millia Islamia
JNU	Jawaharlal Nehru University
JRY	Jawahar Rozgar Yojana
LPM	Landless People's Movement
LWL	Landless Women Labour
MAL	Male Agricultural Labour
MARG	Multiple Action Research Group
MHRD	Ministry of Human Resource Development
MLA	Member of Legislative Assembly
MLC	Member of Legislative Council
MMR	Maternal Mortality Ratio
MSY	Mahila Samriddhi Yojana
NABARD	National Bank for Agriculture and Rural Development
NBA	Narmada Bachao Andolan
NCW	National Commission for Women
NCWR	National Commission for Women's Rights
NGO	Non-Governmental Organisation
NIRD	National Institute of Rural Development
NLC	National Land Committee
NLM	National Literacy Mission
NNP	National Nutrition Policy
NORAD	Norwegian Agency for International Development
NOS	National Open School
NPP	National Perspective Plan
NREP	National Rural Employment Programme
NSAP	National Social Assistance Programme
NSSO	National Sample Survey Organisation
NVTI	National Vocational Training Institute
OBC	Other Backward Classes
PITA	Prevention of Immoral Traffic in women and girls Act

PMIUPEP	Prime Minister's Integrated Urban Poverty Eradication Programme
PMLA	Pariwarik Mahila Lok Adalat
PMRY	Prime Minister's Rozgar Yojana
PNDT	Pre-Natal Diagnostic Techniques
PRI	Panchayat Raj Institution
RDSN	Rural Development Services Network
RLE	Rural Labour Estimates
RLEGP	Rural Landless Employment Guarantee Programme
RMK	Rashtriya Mahila Kosh
RVTI	Regional Vocational Training Institute
RWDEP	Rural Women's Development and Empowerment Project
SAARC	South Asian Association for Regional Cooperation
SC/ST	Scheduled Castes / Scheduled Tribes
SEEUY	Scheme for Employment of Educated Unemployed Youth
SEPUP	Self-Employment Programme for the Urban Poor
SEWA	Self-Employed Women's Association
SHG	Self-Help Group
SPSS	Statistical Package for Social Sciences
SITA	Suppression of Immoral Traffic in women and girls Act
SGSY	Swarnajayanti Gram Swarozgar Yojana
SJSRY	Swarna Jayanti Shahari Rozgar Yojana
SNCWS	Sarojini Naidu Centre for Women Studies (JMI)
TOI	Times of India
TRYSEM	Training for Rural Youth for Self-Employment
UBSP	Urban Basic Services for the Poor
UN	United Nations
UNDP	United Nations Development Programme

UNESCO	United Nations Educational, Scientific and Cultural Organisation
UNHCHR	United Nations High Commissioner for Human Rights
UNHCR	United Nations High Commissioner for Refugees
UNIDO	United Nations Industrial Development Organisation
UNIFEM	United Nation's Development Fund for Women
UP	Uttar Pradesh
WCP	Women Component Plan
WDC	Women's Development Corporation
WDP	Women Development Programme
WHO	World Health Organisation
WPR	Work Participation Rate

LIST OF TABLES

Chapter 1

INTRODUCTION

Landless unorganised female labour force is probably the most miserable section of society. They work on the farms of others during season. Rest of the time they remain unemployed. They form highly marginalised and extremely deprived group which is excluded from the mainstream society. When we study labour ratio we find that in India 97 per cent labour force is unorganised. According to the statistics only 4.2 per cent women work in organised sector. The distribution of female work participation by status of employment shows that 57 per cent of the women in rural areas are self-employed, 2.1 per cent are regular employees and 40.9 per cent are working as casual labours. They keep on changing the occupation but most of the time they work as landless labours (NSSO, 1997).

Number of surveys and studies conducted on agricultural labours indicate that this is one of the most important areas which generates employment in rural areas especially among women. According to Census 1991, over 64 per cent of all main earners work in agriculture. Women main earners (79 per cent) work in agriculture out of which 45 per cent are agriculture labours. Cultivators constitute the next largest share. However, percentage of female workers amongst cultivators is 29.13. It shows that women work on land despite that, they seldom own the resources and majority of them are landless labours. They have limited access to other supportive resources like credit, technology and training and it also shows the ratio of male and female workers in major sectors (Table 1.1).

According to NSSO 55th round, 84 per cent of the women in rural areas and 14.6 per cent in urban areas are engaged in agriculture. Studies conducted in other countries have also reached at the similar conclusion. Maximum number of women are engaged in agriculture followed by manufacturing and processing in household industry (Table 1.1). The higher ratio of landless women labours in the unskilled and labour intensive agricultural operations is a proof for lower status of women in the domains of work. The participation of women in the skilled and technical occupations is lower than that of men (NSSO, 2000).

Table 1.1 : Ratio of female and male workers in major sectors.

Activity	*Female/male workers (%)*
Agricultural labour	62.16
Manufacturing in household industry	49.08
Cultivators	29.13
Livestock, forestry, fishing etc.	23.45
Mining and quarrying	14.16
Manufacturing in other than household industry	12.70
Construction	8.35
Trade and commerce	7.32
Transport, storage and communication	2.67
Other services	22.26

Source : Census of India, 1991.

Status of Landless Women Labours Across the World

Landless women labours around the world do not enjoy an equal status or privileges as compared to men. According to International Fund for Agriculture Development (IFAD) study under the Gender Strengthen Programme for Eastern and Southern Africa, agriculture is found to be the main occupation of rural households in Uganda, especially of the womenfolk. All employed women (72 %) and all rural women (90 %) work in agriculture whereas only 53 per cent of rural men do so (IFAD, 2000). The Statistics Division of Economics and Social Department of FAO provides a host of gender-segregated data in agriculture presented in Table 1.2.

Table 1.2 : Share of female in agriculture labour force in total agriculture population.

Attributes	*1950*	*1970*	*1990*	*2000 (est.)*	*2010 (est.)*
Agriculture Population in world	1,621,927	2,001,885	2,465,015	2,601,722	2,667,219
Share of agriculture population of developing countries	81.39	90.28	94.50	96.09	97.12
Share of female labour force of developing countries	68.40	69.09	73.53	75.83	78.29
Female agriculture labour force in the world	315,924	382,605	523,315	579,771	621,308
Share of female labour force of the developing countries	82.17	89.86	95.43	97.01	97.98
World	39.01	41.13	42.69	43.55	44.16
Developed	41.07	43.77	38.88	36.13	33.73
Developing	38.59	40.85	42.93	43.83	44.44
Share of agriculture labour force in total labour force	89.56	84.21	75.97	70.62	65.21
Share of female labour force in agriculture labour force	44.70	45.87	47.34	48.10	48.74

Source : Food and Agriculture Organisation, 2000.

So even at the global level, agriculture is the most important area which generates employment especially among women and in developing countries. Women farmers grow at least half of the world's food and upto 80 per cent in some African countries. They are responsible for gathering an even larger share of food consumed by their own families: in sub-Saharan Africa (80 %), in Asia (65 %) and 45 per cent in Latin America and the Caribbean (USDA, 2000).

Further, women comprise between one-third and one-half of all agricultural labours in developing countries. For example, African women perform about 90 per cent of the work of processing food crops and 80 per cent of the work of harvesting and marketing. Despite their significant role, women do not share equally with men in the rewards from agriculture, nor are they always beneficiaries of presumed improvements in agricultural technologies and practices. Often, they cannot own or inherit the land on which they work and frequently have difficulty in obtaining improved seeds or fertilisers available to male farmers.

As a rule, women farmers work longer hours and have lower incomes than do male farmers. This is not because they are less educated or less competent. Rather, it is due to restricting socio-cultural factors. Firstly, most women farmers are involved in subsistence farming or food production for the local market that yields little cash return. Secondly, they have less access to credit at bank than men. Government-subsidised rates that would make it possible for them to acquire the 'Green Revolution' technology, such as hybrid seeds and fertilisers are also comparatively inaccessible to women. Thirdly, in some societies women cannot own land and so are excluded from agricultural improvement programmes and projects aimed at landowners. For example, many African agricultural development programmes are based on the conversion of communal land to private holdings. This conversion adversely affects women because women have access to communal land while they are excluded from private holdings.

In Asia, inheritance laws favour male over female heirs, and female-inherited land is managed by husbands. In Latin America, discrimination results from the more limited status held by women under the law. At the same time, the 'Green Revolution' and its greater commercialisation of crops has generally required an increase in labour per hectare, particularly in tasks typically reserved for women such as weeding, harvesting, and post-harvest work. If women are provided no relief from their other daily tasks, the 'Green Revolution' for them may be more burden than blessing.

When mechanisation is introduced to the new farming system, women tend to be losers. Frequently, such predominantly female tasks as harvesting or de-husking and polishing of grain—all traditionally done by hand—are given over to machinery, depriving rather than employing women. Even the application of chemical fertilisers (a man's task) instead of cow dung (women's work) has reduced the female role in agricultural development programmes.

The loss of those traditional female wage jobs means that the rural women and their families who are otherwise poor, have insufficient income to improve their diets even in the light of substantial increase in food availability through 'Green Revolution'.

In India a comparison of two Rural Labour Estimates (1964-65 to 1974-75) show that the estimated number of female agricultural labours in the households has increased over this period. Agriculture labours increased from 30.8 to 46.4 per cent, Female Agricultural Labours (FAL) from 11.5 to 18.3 per cent and Male Agricultural Labours (MAL) from 17.5 to 25.2 per cent respectively. The percentage of agriculture labour households underwent increases from 21.79 to 25.27 million. The report also noted that in the countryside as a whole more than 50 per cent of the rural households did not possess land.

A study conducted in Nigeria, financed by the United Nations Development Programme (UNDP) in 1987 reveals that women make up 60-80 per cent of the agricultural labour force in Nigeria and produce two-thirds of the food crops. Yet, men and not women, make the key farm management decisions. As a result, agricultural extension services in Nigeria (as in other African countries) have traditionally been focused on men and their farm production needs, while neglecting the female half of the production force (www.undp.org).

United States presents a better picture of female agricultural labours. Approximately 40 per cent of all private agricultural land in the United States was owned solely by women (Rogers and Vandeman, 1993). According to the US Department of Agriculture's Economic Research Service (the most recent Census of agriculture data available):

(1) Women operated 145,200 farms, about 7.5 per cent of the US total. The average size of these farms was 309 acres.
(2) Average age of a female farm operator in the US is 58 years.
(3) Women operators (78 %) were full owners of their farms (USDA, 1998).

In British Columbia and Canada, approximately 35 per cent of all farm operators were women. USDA's Farm Service Agency has increased the amount of money lent to women farmers by 65 per cent since 1995. This percentage represents an additional 1,702 loans made to women for maintaining or expanding their farm.

Gender Based Division of Labour

Rural Indian women are extensively involved in agricultural activities. However, the nature and extent of their involvement differs with the variations in agro-production systems. Women's traditional jobs in agriculture are to transplant, sow, weed, harvest, winnow and thresh. The mode of female participation in agricultural production varies with the land-owning status of farm households. Their roles range from managers to landless labours. In overall farm production, women's average contribution is estimated at 55 to 66 per cent of the total labour with percentages much higher in certain regions. In the Indian Himalayas a pair of bullocks works 1064 hours, a man 1212 hours and a woman 3485 hours in a year on a one-hectare farm, a figure which illustrates women's significant contribution to agricultural production (Venkateswaran, 1992).

Women provide one half of the labour in rice cultivation in India. In the plantation sector, women are the crucial labours. Depending on the region and crops, women's contributions vary but they provide pivotal labour from planting to harvesting and post-harvest operations. Traditionally, women had rights to the community land. But after the land reforms, land titles were given to men, denying women's access to land. In general, women in tribal households enjoy more decision-making power than women in many other Indian households because of their greater contribution to household income. So far as wages are concerned women are again discriminated. Like any other occupation, wage discrimination is equally prevalent in agriculture (Nagaraj, 1988).

We can see from the Table 1.3, that among wage workers in rural areas, wage discrimination is very much frequent as reported by National Commission on Labour, (2002).

Table 1.3 : Rural agriculture wage earnings among wage workers in Rural Labour Households at 1960-61 prices.

Year	*Adult male*	*Adult female*
1964-65	1.0	0.6
1974-75	0.9	0.6
1977-78	1.2	0.8
1983	1.0	0.7
1987-88	1.4	1.1
1993-94	1.9	1.3

Source : National Commission on Labour, GOI, 2002.

Discrimination in female agriculture employment is mainly due to the division of labour based on sex. Female labour is primarily involved in specific operations such as transplanting, weeding, harvesting and threshing. In contrast, male labour is much more evenly spread across operations and this is found to be across different states and crops (Agarwal, 1994).

Problems of Landless Women Labours

Land is the most important economic factor of production. Its ownership reflects the economic power structure within the society which guarantees access to important agriculture inputs. Women are mostly denied their right to own land. Even when women hold legal titles to land, they often lack control over it or the revenues it generates. Some historians believe that it was woman who first domesticated crop plants and thereby initiated the art and science of farming. While men went out in search of food, women started gathering seed from the native flora and began cultivating. They did this from the point of view of food, feed, fodder, fibre and fuel (Swaminathan, 1985). Today women constitute the largest group of landless labours with little security in case of break up of family due to death or divorce. Inheritance laws and customs discriminate against them.

Women's lack of ownership is an indication of the extent to which they are relegated to an inferior position in society. On the economic front, the lack of owning land effectively precludes women from access to a number of agricultural support services, because land is most often used as collateral by many banks and developmental organisations to disburse loans and agricultural input. They are simply perceived as supplementary and are not granted recognition as farmers. This is the group, which not only highly impoverish but also represents feminisation of poverty.

Landless labours, especially women, are involved in most precarious and least rewarding works. They form an extremely poor group of people who are not sure of next meal. Nearly 1.3 billion people all over the world are suffering from persistence hunger and poverty. Strangely enough 70 per cent of them are women. As payment to women workers is less than the wages of their male counterparts, usually they are at the bottom as far as economic status is concerned.

Bonded Labour

An extreme manifestation of sorry plight of agricultural labours is the bonded labour system. This system is rampant in Indian agriculture sector. It thrives under different names in different states. The bonded labour system took deep roots in the regions where schedule castes, schedule tribes, adivasi and other depressed classes abound. According to the final report of National Survey on the incidence of bonded labour, in the State of Andhra Pradesh, the places of high incidence of bonded labour are Karimnagar, Mehboobnagar, Medak, Nalgonda, Nizamabad and Warrangal. In these places they are popularly known as *Jeetham, Paalithanam* and *Vettichakiri*. Followed by Bihar, Maharashtra, Orissa and Madhya Pradesh show equally high incidence of bonded labour in agriculture. Among the bonded agricultural labours, majority are landless women.

Migration

Migration is an inevitable condition for economic development.

People move away from the dwindling opportunities of the remote villages to the expanding or expected opportunities at prosperous rural or urban centres. But the migration of agriculture labour is a negation to the common meaning of migration for economic prosperity. The migration being the last alternative exposes them to various kind of exploitation and proves to be a bane rather than a boon. Poverty, unemployment, underemployment, and low wages drive them to move towards urban areas and prosperous rural areas like Punjab and Haryana. The trend of highest rate of migration is featured in adult landless agricultural labours and marginal farmers. In comparison to rural-urban, rural-migration is much higher. The push and pull factors for migration are almost same.

A survey of five villages in Ludhiana about the migrant labours to Punjab revealed that the multiple factors that forced the migrant labours to move to Punjab were to earn their living, poverty, unemployment and non-availability of regular work in their native places, low wages, social discrimination and persecution by caste Hindus and frequent floods and droughts. The minimum wages fixed in these states are higher than that in their states of origin. In such conditions the uprooted poor migrants are easily exploited by the landowners. Discriminatory wages, unregulated working hours, payment of wages less than the minimum wages and wrong calculation etc. are some of the common malpractices. All these factors affect worse the women compared to the men.

Unorganised Nature of Work

In India more than 90 per cent of the total workforce are engaged in unorganised sector, of which majority are in agriculture. The economic backwardness of agricultural labours is due to several factors such that they have been neglected by social workers, political leaders and the government and their wages are not revised regularly. The actual cause for such a sorry state is non-implementation of governmental measures on one hand and the absence of organised pressure from the workers on the other hand.

The organisation of rural poor can play a crucial role in

transforming the situation by providing a new power base. The political influence and the economic hegemony of the rural elite are often so inextricably interlocked that they tend to become a closed, almost monolithic power structure. It does not encourage any meaningful dialogue or effective cooperation with those who live in the periphery of rural community. Consequently the unorganised landless agricultural labours get easily victimised and exploited. Women labours are again the worst affected group.

Illiteracy and Exploitation

The effect of education on development and *vice versa* becomes clearly discernible in the estimation of illiterates on world planes. The vast majority of illiterates, amounting to almost three quarter of the total are to be found in Asia. Africa has one-fifth of the total illiterate population, while the remaining are in Latin America. In India the maximum concentration of illiterates is in rural areas and that too amongst socially and economically depressed masses. Majority of them are marginal farmers and agricultural labours. It has been calculated that 94.2 per cent of India's rural population have no skill and the incidence of rural illiteracy is high. Women join agricultural employment without any understanding of the concept of wage employment.

Casualisation of Landless Women Labour

The pattern and trends in employment show a trend towards casualisation, i.e. an increase in the number of casual worker, both male and female in rural areas. However, casual workforce forms a large proportion of women workforce as compared to their male counterparts. Also the trend of casualisation both for females and males has been more in rural areas as compared to urban areas. In rural areas, the proportion of casual labour, both male and female has increased phenomenally. The share of casual labour among females is much higher than males. This means that a large number of women agricultural workers have no permanent jobs, their work is seasonal and they are not employed on all days of month.

According to Unni (1999) a large proportion of landless and semi-landless persons work as casual wage labours. Increase in landless households and precariously small holdings add to the pressure on casual labour wage market. She also highlights that while men in landless households are able to find other kind of works, women in such households are only confined to wage work. An option of diversification to non-agriculture employment, which is better paying, is increasingly limited for women.

The relationship between female Work Productivity Rate (WPR) and the extent of casualisation of the workforce is much higher. The correlation co-efficient is 0.42 for all the 12 states for which data are available such as Maharashtra, Andhra Pradesh, Tamil Nadu, Gujarat, Madhya Pradesh, Rajasthan, Punjab, Haryana, Uttar Pradesh, Bihar, West Bengal and Kerala (Census of India, 1981). On the other hand studies show strong inverse relationship between female WPR and the link with the land. This strong inverse relationship between links with land and female WPR and a strong positive relation between landlessness and female WPR clearly indicates the deteriorating status of female agriculture labours.

Health Hazards of Landless Women Labours

The work processes women agriculture workers are involved in have severe and specific effect on their health. Manual planting and sowing involve uncomfortable postures. The working methods and implements in farming are often traditional where concern for the well-being and comfort of women was as distant as it is now. Several studies have shown a symbolic relationship between women's work in agriculture and their reproductive health. One indicator of the adverse consequences of such work is relatively high child mortality, especially where paddy cultivation dominates (Swaminathan, 1997). An earlier study in an agriculture area in Maharashtra showed that during the month of transplanting operations women work in a squatting posture all the day long and there was found a very strong clustering of child deaths. Over 37 per cent of deaths occurred in these months (Batliwala, 1983).

According to a case study reported in the State of Madhya Pradesh, women used to carry a metal vessel containing seed grain mixed with fertiliser powder in the operation of sowing. The vessel usually weighs 3 to 4 kg. and is suspended against their abdomen by straps from their shoulders. Women experience great difficulty due to heavy load, long distance and the posture of arm required for sowing the seeds. For the operation of weeding, the women assume a sitting posture and crawl forward slowly inch by inch to pull out the grass or cut the bigger plants. The posture during harvesting work causes great strain on muscles of the back and legs. Backache and leg pain are the most common problems of landless women workers.

Recent technological advancements in cultivation methods have led to new risks for women workers. Some of the chemical products used for weeding, controlling plant diseases and eradicating tests for insects are known to be harmful for those handling them. Chemicals like DDT, Endrine, Malathion and Benzene hex-acholoride (BHC) used in agricultural operations affect not only the respiratory system, but also the optic nerve and reproductive organs. A high incidence of tuberculosis, bronchial ailments, loss of eyesight, including injury to optical nerves, foetal injury and other hazards have been noted in tea plantations. Lung infections and bronchial troubles are also common (ILO, 1983).

Needless to say that the most serious problems, the landless women labour face are the sexual and work place harassment. Since majority of them are illiterate, they prefer to remain silent and very often they admit these happenings as part of their normal lifestyle. The study under consideration examines the plight of the landless women labours in Delhi, Uttar Pradesh and Haryana.

Chapter 2

REVIEW OF LITERATURE

Women are the invisible and unrecognised backbone of the agriculture. Despite their critical involvement and contribution in agriculture, their presence is officially unseen, with few statistics reflecting their actual contribution to agricultural output and rural employment, and thereby to the Gross Domestic Product. Many women work on small landholdings in subsistence agriculture where very little output is sold in the market. Most women are landless labours and work as casual wage earners. Agricultural workers are the lowest paid employment segment in whole of South Asia, and women receive the lowest remuneration within the sector. Especially when landless women seek employment on other farms, they are met with low demands. In general, they perform those very tasks, which are low paid. In India's rural areas, women dominated activities like weeding but are paidless.

Several studies have been conducted on the status of landless women labours. Different aspects of the landless labours have been highlighted in these studies such as phenomenon of landlessness, casualisation, wage differentials, mechanisation of agriculture and rising unemployment, health hazards and other associated problems of these labourers.

The relevant literature has been reviewed in the following categories:

- The phenomenon of landlessness and casualisation of labour.
- Gender based division of labour and wage differentials in agriculture.
- Mechanisation of agriculture and rising unemployment
- Associated problems of landless women agricultural labours.

The Phenomenon of Landlessness and Casualisation of Labour

A study conducted in Nigeria and financed by the United Nations Development Programme (UNDP) reveals that women make up 60-80 per cent of the agricultural labour force in Nigeria and produce two-thirds of the food crops. Yet, men make the key farm management decisions. As a result, agricultural extension services in Nigeria (as in other African countries) have traditionally been focused on men and their farm production needs, while neglecting the female half of the production force (www.undp.org).

Nagraj (1988) in his preliminary study on female workers in rural Tamil Nadu shows a strong inverse relationship between female Work Participation Rate (WPR) and the link with land. The female WPR (Work Participation Rate) is the lowest for cultivating castes who obviously have strongest relationship with land. The other castes appear to have the weakest link with land, with none of them reporting cultivation as occupation. This strong inverse relationship between links with land and the female WPR or a strong positive relation between landlessness and female WPR shows the deteriorating status of women labours in agriculture.

Punia (1992) in his book *Women in Agriculture* quotes that "it was women who first domesticated crop plants and thereby initiated the art and science of farming. While men went out searching in hunt of food, women started gathering seed from the native flora and began cultivating those of interest from the point of view of food, feed, fodder, fibre and fuel." He further observes that inspite of this fact, women are the largest group of landless labour with little security in case of break up of family, owing to death or divorce, inheritance laws and customs dominate against them.

Venkateswaran (1992), in his book *Living on the Edge: Women, Environment and Development,* discusses the status of rural women in India. They are extensively involved in agricultural activities. However, the nature and extent of their involvement differs with the variations in agro-production systems. The mode of female participation in agricultural production varies with the land-owning status of farm households. Their roles range from managers to landless labours. In overall farm production, women's average contribution is estimated at 55 to 66 per cent of the total labour with percentages much higher in certain regions.

Rogers and Vandeman (1993) in their article *Women Farm Landlords in the United States* presents a better scenario about women in agriculture in developed countries. Approximately 40 per cent of all private agricultural land in the United States was owned solely by women.

Sharma and Singh (1993) discuss in the book entitled *Women and Work; Changing Scenario in India,* the detailed surveys of rural landless labouring households in Tamil Nadu, Kerala, West Bengal and elsewhere show the share of earned income contributed to the households by wives and husbands. Women contribute a much higher percentage of their incomes. The findings for the Tamil Nadu show that:

(1) In Thanjavur, wives contributed 99 per cent and husbands 77 per cent.
(2) In South Arcot wives contributed 97 per cent and husbands 79 per cent.

She quoted that: "What is most significant in these figures is that in every case, the proportion of income contributed by wage earning women to the household is far higher than that of their earning husbands".

According to Census, 1991, more than 190 million workers out of 314 million total workers were engaged in unorganised sector. Agricultural labours accounted for nearly 40 per cent of the agricultural workforce. Almost the entire workforce engaged in agriculture, forestry, fishery and plantation are unorganised. Even in the nineteenth century census operations, the colonial administration did not recognise the agricultural labours as a separate category of workers and all their problems were addressed in sections allocated for slavery. For quite sometime, the British considered that it was 'natural' for Indians to have such slave labours and avoided their rights and resistance. Only after the development of colonial capitalism accompanied by Europe's discussion on 'abolition of slavery' and 'emancipation', the British started showing interest in generating information on agricultural labours as a separate social entity. The changes in Indian religions which rejected slavery as an institution also played a considerable role. Thanks to the struggles of the Indian masses, legislations were enacted.

Unni (1999) has studied about the relationship between landlessness and casualisation. A large proportion of landless and semi-landless persons work as casual wage labours. So increase in landlessness has given rise to another phenomenon of casualisation of labour.

Nicole Itano in an article entitled *Despite Promises Zimbabwean Women Not Given Land*, highlights the loopholes in the legislation itself. Agriculture in traditional Southern African societies is largely women's work. Women compose 52 per cent of the Zimbabwean population, yet they provide 70 per cent of the country's agricultural labour, according to the Food and Agriculture Organisation of the United Nations. Women also tend to be more dependent on agriculture for survival, with an estimated 86 per cent of women working the land (Itano, 2002). Men often migrate to cities and to the mines, leaving their wives to care for their families in villages and to grow a small crop of corn, the region's staple food. But women in Zimbabwe, particularly in communal areas, have few rights to the land they work. Land is usually passed from father to son and a wife has little claim to that land after the death of her husband. The Zimbabwe Constitution theoretically protects women's rights to land ownership as inheritance; however, the country's Supreme Court ruled in 1999 that African customary law superseded the constitution and that a woman could not challenge her brother's claim to their father's land. Promises by the government in October, 2000 were that 20 per cent of redistributed land would go to female-headed households raised expectations among women's groups in Zimbabwe. Till date, there has been no governmental effort to ensure that women are indeed benefiting from the land-reform process and the land quota for women has not been put into statute (www.research.umbc.edu).

Gender Based Division of Labour and Wage Differentials in Agriculture

Discrimination in female agriculture employment is mainly due to the division of labour based on sex. Female labour is primarily involved in specific operations such as transplanting, weeding, harvesting and threshing. In contrast, male labour is much more evenly spread across operations. This is found to be different across various states and crops (Sharma and Singh, 1993).

The wage discrimination is a consequence of poverty and illiteracy of agricultural labour, the casual nature of employment and ignorance of law, all of which apply particularly to the women. As per Minimum Wages Act, 1948 (2nd Schedule) minimum wages are to be fixed by State Governments for agricultural labours and the rates are to be reviewed periodically at intervals not exceeding five years. There are still some states, which have not brought large area of agriculture employment within the ambit of this Act. The machinery for fixation and enforcement of minimum wages is not uniform (Verma, 1993).

According to NSSO report, 31.5 per cent of total agriculture work is done by men and the remaining 68.5 per cent by women (Table 2.1).

Table 2.1 : Works done by men and women in agriculture.

Work done by men	*Work done by women*
Tilling and preparing land	Making seeds beds
Sowing seeds	Plugging and transplanting sapling
Cutting crops and carrying crops home	Lifting weeds
Selling in market and collection of money	Harvesting
Decisive roles	Threshing
	Boiling paddy

Source : NSSO 50th Round, 1994.

The NSSO data shows that women are doing three fourth work of all the agriculture, which is exhausting, time consuming, requiring the least use of technology and decision-making. The work is seasonal for large number of women in agriculture and they are not employed on all the days of month (NSSO, 1994).

The National Commission on labour mentions the continuation of wage differentials in agriculture between men and women and had observed that "In the large sector where women are employed, *viz.* agriculture and small industries, evidence shows that in fixing wage rates, some state governments are not free from showing discrimination against women." Table 2.2 clearly indicates the differences in maximum and minimum wages of men and women for same agriculture operation in Uttar Pradesh (Jain, *et. al.*, 1997).

Table 2.2 : Differences in Wages in Uttar Pradesh.

	Maximum	*Minimum*
Sowers	—	—
Men	66.56	11.27
Women	47.70	9.75
Weeders	—	—
Men	60.0	11.23
Women	42.80	10.16
Reapers	—	—
Men	52.60	8.87
Women	42.85	8.07

Source : Directorate of Economic Statistics, Ministry of Agriculture, Government of India, 1972

Apart from differences in wages for the same jobs, discrimination against women is exemplified also by the fact that they are usually engaged in traditionally lower ranking jobs, viz. sowing, weeding, transplanting, winnowing, threshing and harvesting as against ploughing which is done mostly by men.

The Study Group on Women and Child Labour reports that women wage workers in the agriculture sector earns substantially lower wages than their counterparts (Unni, 1999).

Unemployment and Mechanisation of Labour

According to *Shramshakti* Report of National Commission on Self-employed Women and Women in Informal Sector, most of the women in agriculture were constantly trying to find some other sources of income to tide them over in the off season. Women in North East, H. P., Jammu and Kashmir and Tamil Nadu do weaving during the off-season. Many agricultural labours in Gujarat, Maharashtra, U.P. and Karnataka take up work with road construction crews in the off-season. Some work with weavers, or khadi spinners or tassar reelers (GOI, 1988).

Binita Verma (1993) discusses the problem of unemployment among landless labours. Seasonal unemployment is the manifestation of rural poverty where individuals are forced to take on low productivity jobs, which do not always ensure minimum subsistence. The female landless labours form an important but weak segment of rural population.

Subhasini Mahapatra (2002) comments regarding the impact of mechanisation on landless women agricultural labours. There is growing number of agricultural labours because of the population growth and also decrease in the availability of work because of increased use of farm machinery. Studies in India and the third world countries show the effect mechanisation of post-harvest activities has on poor landless women.

Rai (2002) makes a comparative analysis of mechanisation of agriculture in different countries. In countries like India, Bangladesh and Malaysia, labour saving devices have been introduced much faster than in other Asian countries like Japan. Complete mechanisation of rice farming in Japan came about only in the 1970s much after the introduction of new labour intensive techniques and rise of yields. Today mechanical devices are already available from developed countries and being used in developing countries, which have a very large number of landless labours. The result is that farmers' opportunities to substitute labour by capital are far greater than opportunities to substitute capital by labour.

Health Hazards of the Agriculture

ILO studies highlight the health hazard of the work processes women agriculture workers are involved in, which have a specific and severe effect on their health. Manual planting and sowing involves uncomfortable postures. The working methods and implements are often the legacy of the past, or product of local customs or traditions, where concern for the well-being and comfort of women was as distant as it is now (ILO, 1983).

A study in an agriculture area in Maharashtra showed how during the month of transplanting operations, when women do work in a squatting posture all day long, for up to 12 hours, there was a very strong clustering of child deaths. Over 37 per cent of deaths occurred in these months (Batliwala, 1983).

WHO estimate in mid 1980s shows that India accounted for about one-third or more of all cases (500,000 cases every year) of pesticides' poisoning in the underdeveloped countries. In the mid-1980s, 70 per cent of the total agro-chemicals used in India were either banned or their use severely restricted in the developed countries. Recent technological advancements in cultivation methods have led to new risks for women workers. A high incidence of tuberculosis, bronchial ailments, loss of eyesight, including injury to optical nerves, foetal injury and other hazards have been noted in tea plantations.

Swaminathan has shown a symbolic relation between women's work in agriculture and their reproductive health. One indicator of the adverse consequences of such work is relatively high child mortality, especially where paddy cultivation dominates (Swaminathan, 1997).

Concluding Remarks

It can be seen from the above stated reviews that several studies are held on the problems of the landless labours and women. No specific study is held on the empowerment problems of landless women such as sexual and work place harassment, inequality in wages, gender discrimination at home, lack of ownership of property, and rights over own earnings by the working women and many others. Labour legislations were beneficial to regular employees. The landless women being nomadic labour force are engaged partly in the fields and partly at the construction sites and they hardly avail the benefits of social security measures. The illiteracy and the lack of productive skills keep the landless women labours, casual and unskilled workers giving them little opportunity for an alternative occupation. Seasonal nature of the agricultural works compels the agricultural workers to migrate to the cities temporarily. They seldom get chance to continue any occupation over six months' duration. The problems faced by women in these circumstances are seldom reported. Hence this study is conducted.

Chapter 3

WOMEN LANDLES LABOUR IN INDIA

(POLICIES AND PROGRAMMES)

There are several government and non-governmental initiatives to mitigate the problems of landless women labours. This chapter highlights the Government policies, welfare schemes, and legislative procedures that affect the landless women labours in India. It is also important to understand the role of civil society and NGOs. All these aspects have been explained comprehensively in this chapter.

The Five Year Plans

The Five Year Plans give special emphasis to the present situation of agricultural labours. The programmes under the *First Five Year Plan* (1951-1956) aimed at increasing agricultural production substantially. Extension of irrigation, intensive cultivation and improvement in agricultural practices have increased rural employment and thus afforded greater opportunity to agricultural workers.

Provision of Land

Through measures related to land reform many tenants, who are also in some part agricultural labours, have obtained security and greater protection and came on the way to becoming owners. Some land especially that which is not now under the cultivation of tenants, was also available for agricultural workers. It will be recalled that in making proposals for the reorganisation of the rural economy on co-operative lines, one of the major objects in view is to carry out changes, which will rapidly place the agricultural worker in a position of equality in status and opportunity with other sections of the village community. Since the 1950's five year plans there has been a gradual improvement in the status of agricultural production and the agricultural labours.

As the economy as a whole develops, an increasing number of workers will be drawn away from the village, so that both those who move out of the village and those who remain in the village are likely to obtain more adequate employment. In addition to the industrial programmes in the Plan and those relating to transport and other fields of economic life, the Plan contains important programmes for village industries and the promotion of khadi. These will be of direct benefit to agricultural workers.

Agricultural labour populations are mostly concentrated in areas where population presses heavily on the land and the development in sectors of the economy other than the agriculture has been retarded. By selecting such areas for special programmes such as community development projects, it should be possible to make a distinct contribution to the problem of rehabilitating agricultural workers, for an increase in the tempo of development is the effective answer to the problem of unemployment and under-employment.

Focus on Lower Caste People

While a number of different programmes were implemented in the *Third Five Year Plan* to promote the interests of agricultural workers, special mention may be made of the assistance set apart for the amelioration of backward classes. This assistance was for the resettlement schemes for landless agricultural workers. Some initiatives were taken to liberate the bonded agricultural labours who were mostly women of scheduled caste. Assistance was given to the State Governments to identify and liberate the landless and bonded women labours belonging to the scheduled castes and resettle them by allotting agricultural land in identified areas. This resettlement scheme had included assistance for construction of houses too. However, the scheme was not found effective in many of the states due to apathy and indifference on the part of the State Government.

House Sites

During the Fourth FiveYear Plan tenancy reforms received a renewed attention. Efforts were initiated as a continuation of the action started during the Third Five Year Plan, to allot housing sites for the landless labours within the land premises where they had been working for generations. Agricultural workers, not being owners of land in a village, were seldom the owners of the sites on which their houses are constructed. This made them dependent on the consent either of individual owners of land or of village proprietary bodies. The scheme for the resettlement provided for allotting independent housing sites for the landless labours.

This scheme had also several limitations. Since the house sites were far from the work site, the landless women labours had problems in settling down in remote places. In order to get maximum benefit of any resettlement schemes for the landless labours several suggestions are given. Landless workers holding temporary rights over house-sites in a village should be granted rights of occupancy in them. Where the house-sites are the common property of a village, the village panchayat should be placed under obligation to grant the sites free of charge to agricultural workers who may be in occupation of them. The sites should be transferred free of charge to the landless workers either by obtaining these by way of gift from the owners in question or by settling directly with the owners.

Full support should be given to the movement initiated by Acharya Vinoba Bhave for securing land gifts for the landless by providing means of cultivation and other assistance to landless labours selected for the allotment of the gifted land. The movement has considerable moral value and, if pressed forward, holds promise of relief in meeting some of the urgent problems of landless workers. The State Governments could make it a permanent feature of the work of rural development, which might continue beyond the pioneering phase.

Labour Co-operatives

With the assistance of the co-operative staff, the irrigation, buildings and roads, forest and agricultural departments and other government agencies in the states should try and organise co-operatives of village labours. Under the technical guidance of their officials, these co-operatives should be encouraged and enabled to take up contracts for specific pieces of construction work. The success of forest labours' societies in Bombay and of certain other similar efforts elsewhere suggests that, given suitable encouragement and assistance, the formation of labour co-operatives can make an important contribution to the relief of rural unemployment and, in addition, make it possible for the government to assist more adequately with social welfare schemes and other ameliorative measures.

Resettlement Schemes for Landless Workers

Blocks of newly reclaimed land as well as cultivable waste land should be set apart, wherever possible, for the settlement on co-operative lines of groups of landless agricultural workers and of holders of small, uneconomic plots of land. Even though the amount of land which could be thus made available would be limited and the proportion of agricultural workers who could be benefited might be small, the existence of such a scheme in each state could become a source of hope and encouragement in the lives of many families of agricultural workers and would go far to arouse confidence and enterprise in them. Within the scope of the programmes included in the Plan, there is considerable opportunity for organising co-operative settlements and colonisation schemes for agricultural workers and, as a matter of policy, the fullest use should be made of these possibilities. As already mentioned, the Plan makes a special financial provision to promote resettlement schemes for agricultural workers.

Being without land, agricultural workers have no security to offer. As a rule, therefore, they do not become eligible for financial assistance from the Government. While individual loans may present certain administrative difficulties, we suggest that State Governments should formulate schemes for granting financial assistance to co-operative groups of landless workers for such purposes as house building, purchase of bullocks and implements and for ancillary industries which they may wish to take up after suitable training under the auspices of government. Special assistance by way of educational stipends and for vocational and technical training should also be offered, as indeed is already being done in many states.

Welfare Schemes for Agriculture Labour

Apart from the various provisions of Five Year Plans, there are number of welfare schemes for the rural population which would invariably benefit the agricultural labours. Some of them have been mentioned below:

- Group Insurance Scheme for Landless Agricultural Labour operated by Insurance Division, Ministry of Finance.
- Group Life Insurance Scheme for IRDP beneficiaries operated by Department of Rural Development.
- Group Insurance Scheme for Landless Agricultural Labours of the State of Gujarat.
- Asha Kiran Scheme of the Government of Karnataka.
- Insurance-cum-Retirement Benefit Special Scheme for the workers in the unorganised sector of Tamil Nadu Government.
- Scheme for Financial Assistance to Landless Women Agricultural Labours during Pregnancy operated by Gujarat Government.
- Personal Accident Insurance Social Security Scheme for Poor Families.
- Hut Insurance Scheme.

- Kerala Agricultural Workers' Pension Scheme.
- Andhra Pradesh Landless Agricultural Workers' Pension Scheme.
- Old Age Pension (Destitute Agricultural Labours) Scheme of Tamil Nadu.
- Old Age Pension Schemes of other States/Union Territories.
- Universal Health Scheme of 2003.

Employment Assurance Scheme

Employment Assurance Scheme (EAS) was launched on 2nd October, 1993 in 1778 identified backward blocks of different States. The scheme is being implemented in all the rural blocks of the country.

As its name suggests, the primary objective of the EAS is to provide gainful employment during the lean agricultural season in manual work to all able bodied adults in rural areas who are in need and desirous of work, but cannot find it. The work may be either on farm or on other allied operations or on the normal plan/non-plan works during such a period. The secondary objective is the creation of community, social and economic assets for sustained employment and development.

The EAS is open to all adult rural poor who are in need of wage employment. A maximum of two adults per family (the generally expected number of adults in a family) would be provided wage employment, when there is demand during lean agricultural season, subject to availability of funds.

Swarna Jayanti Gram Swarozgar Yojana

Central Government has started Swarna Jayanti Gram Swarozgar Yojana in April 1999. In this scheme IRDP, TRYSEM, *Ganga Kalyan, Jeevan Dhara* and *Unnat* Tool Kit have been merged. The main object of the scheme is to eliminate poverty in rural area. In each block, priority is given to 3 or 4 traditional trades according to the local market and demand. For SC/ST beneficiaries, Rs. 10,000 and others Rs. 7,500 maximum subsidy can be given while for group Rs. 125,000 subsidy amount can be given. The objective of this scheme is to organise the rural poor into self-help groups and build their capacities so that they can start their own income generating ventures.

Jawahar Gram Samridhi Yojana

Jawahar Gram Samridhi Yojana (JGSY) is the restructured, streamlined and comprehensive version of the erstwhile Jawahar Rozgar Yojana. Designed to improve the quality of life of the poor, JGSY has been launched on 1st April, 1999. The primary objective of the JGSY is the creation of demand driven community village infrastructure including durable assets at the village level and assets to enable the rural poor to increase the opportunities for sustained employment. The secondary objective is the generation of supplementary employment for the unemployed poor in the rural areas. The wage employment under the programme shall be given to Below Poverty Line (BPL) families.

JGSY is implemented entirely at the Village Panchayat Level. Village Panchayat is the sole authority for preparation of the Annual Plan and its implementation. The programme is implemented as centrally sponsored scheme on cost sharing basis between the Centre and the State in the ratio of 75:25 respectively.

Training of Rural Youth for Self-Employment (TRYSEM)

The programme aims at providing basic technical and managerial skills to the rural youth from families below the poverty line to enable them to take up self-employment and wage employment in agricultural and allied sectors, industries, services and business activities. Trades like tailoring, automobile, driving, computer, type writing, sericulture, mushroom cultivation, book binding and printing, motor coil rewinding, two-wheeler mechanism and electricians etc. have been included.

Technical entrepreneurial skills are imparted to the rural youth in the age group of 18-35 from families below the poverty line. The minimum age is relaxable to 16 years for inmates of orphanages. In the case of women and bonded labours and convicts, cured leprosy patients and persons displaced by large development programmes, the age relaxation is upto 45 years. TRYSEM is a need-based programme.

It enables them take up income generating activities (self/wage employment). It had been laid down that the coverage of youth from SC/ST communities should be at least 50 per cent of rural youth trained. Out of the total beneficiaries, at least 50 per cent should be women. The scheme had been merged into Swarna Jayanti Gram Swarozgar Yojana (SGSY) with IRDP, DWCRA etc. from April 1999.

Balika Samridhi Yojana

Government of India has launched a new scheme w.e.f. 15.8.1997 for the development of girl child from Below Poverty Line (BPL) families to make them equivalent to boys in the society. Under this scheme scholarship is also given to the girl child from Rs. 300 to 1000 upto the 10th class.

Under this scheme cash assistance of Rs. 500 will be provided to the mothers for nutrition on giving birth to the girl child. Such women should belong to the families below poverty line and this benefit will be restricted to two girl children irrespective of the size of the family. During the year 2000-2001, 100 women have been provided assistance.

Mahila Samakhya

The Mahila Samakhya is a pilot programme of the Department of Education, Ministry of Human Resource Development, Government of India. It was born out of the emphasis given in the New Education Policy of 1986 to the need for education programmes to play a positive, interventionist role in bringing about women's equality.

Despite the many educational and developmental programmes

undertaken by the Government over the past four decades, women remain exploited and oppressed. The worst lot are the poor, rural women who are the most powerless group of all. They play no role in designing the welfare and development schemes but must remain their passive 'beneficiaries.' The objective of Mahila Samakhya is to reverse this process. The basic strategy is the building of village level collectives or "*sanghs*" which are not merely activity oriented but which enable women to improve their self-confidence and recognise their own strengths. Mahila Samakhya has also redefined education and delinked it from literacy per se. It sees education as a dynamic process of learning, where women receive meaningful information, engage in critical reflection and act as a collective to change the living condition.

Women Component Plan (WCP)

The department of Women and Child Welfare extends financial assistance to women and children in difficult circumstances and also to the women and girls to take up job oriented courses. It also imparts training to the women entrepreneurs for widows and other economically weaker section of women. Some special schemes under the WCP are given below:

(1) Educational Scholarship for girls in rural areas.
(2) Financial Assistance to children in difficult circumstances.
(3) Rehabilitation programme for child labour.
(4) Financial Assistance for women to take up job oriented courses.
(5) Jagruthi Scheme for adolescent girls.
(6) Sthree Shakthi Scheme.
(7) Mane Belaku.
(8) Devadasi Rehabilitation Programme.
(9) Udyogini.

Million Wells Scheme (MWS)

Million Wells Scheme was taken up as a sub-scheme of National

Rural Employment Programme (NREP). NREP and Rural Landless Employment Guarantee Programme (RLEGP) continued during the year 1988-89 under Jawahar Rozgar Yojana (JRY). Till 1989-90, the objective of the scheme was to provide open irrigation wells to small and marginal farmers amongst the Scheduled Castes/ Scheduled Tribes and freed Bonded Labours who are below poverty line, free of cost. From 1990-91 onwards, under Million Wells Scheme, the following works were also included :

(a) Construction of open irrigation wells for the target group;
(b) Where wells are not feasible, other scheme of minor irrigation like irrigation tanks, Water Harvesting Structures for the benefit of target group can also be taken up;
(c) The provision under MWS can also be utilised for the land development of the target groups.

From January 1, 1996, this scheme had been delinked from JRY and made an independent scheme by itself. Now the scheme is no more in operation and merged with SGSY since April 1,1999.

Jawahar Rozgar Yojana (JRY)

Alleviation of rural poverty has been one of the main objectives of the development programmes. Since independence various schemes of employment generation were taken up from time to time in the country. The Eighth Plan has also stressed the need for having a larger focus on the programmes aimed at giving self-employment and wage employment to the poorer section of the community. During the first four years of the Seventh Five Year Plan, two Wage-employment Programme *viz.*; National Rural Employment Programme (NREP) and Rural Landless Employment Guarantee Programme (RLEGP) were in operation in the country. From April 1, 1989 i.e. last year of the Seventh Five Year Plan, these programmes were merged into a single wage employment programme known as Jawahar Rozgar Yojana (JRY).

The primary objectives of JRY are generation of additional

gainful employment for the unemployed and under-employed men and women in rural areas. The secondary objectives of this programme are creation of sustainable employment by strengthening the rural economic infrastructure.

Drought Prone Area Programme (DPAP)

The Drought Prone Area Programme (DPAP) aims to mitigate the adverse effect of drought on the production of crops and livestock, productivity of land, water and human resources. It strives to encourage restoration of ecological balance and seeks to improve the economic and social condition of the poor and the disadvantaged sections of the rural community. Now DPAP is a people's programme with government assistance.

There is a specific arrangement for maintenance of assets and social audit by Panchayati Raj Institutions. Development of all categories of land belonging to Gram Panchayat, Government and individuals falls within the limits of the selected watersheds for development. Allocation is to be shared equally by the Centre and State Government on 50:50 basis. Watershed Committee is to contribute for maintenance of the assets created. Utilisation of 50 per cent of allocation under the Employment Assurance Scheme (EAS) is for the Watershed Development Funds are directly released to Watershed Committees and Project Implementing Agencies. Village community including self-help groups can undertake area development projects through Watershed Associations and Watershed Committees constituted from among themselves. The Government supplements their work by creating social awareness imparting trainings and providing technical support through the Project Implementation Agencies.

All these welfare schemes are meant for rural labour. But very few of these schemes are meant for landless women labour that shows the gap in the policy formulation and its implementation. However, if all these schemes are effectively implemented, it can be a significant step for the welfare of women labour in rural areas.

Legislative Provisions

So far as legislative protection is concerned there are 12 laws meant for rural workers most of which are in agricultural sector. Some of these laws are as follows:

- Minimum Wages Act, 1948.
- Plantation Labour Act, 1951.
- The Payment of Wages Act, 1936.
- The Employees State Insurance Act, 1948.
- The Maternity Benefit Act, 1961.
- The Payment of Gratuity Act, 1972.
- The Personal Injuries (Compensation) Act, 1963, and
- The Employees' Provident Fund and Miscellaneous Provisions Act, 1952.

Under the Minimum Wages Act, State Governments are required to fix minimum rates of wages for agricultural labour. The legislation permits them to fix minimum wages for such portions of the territories or for such classes of employment, as they might consider feasible. In most states steps to implement the legislation have already been initiated. In nine states, including Punjab and Uttar Pradesh, minimum wages have been fixed. In Uttar Pradesh minimum wages have already been fixed for farms over 50 acres in twelve districts. In a number of states draft proposals are at present under final scrutiny. Enquiries to ascertain low wage pockets are in progress as in Madras.

The enforcement of minimum wages for agricultural workers in low wage pockets, for the larger farms and in areas selected for intensive development should be regarded as an important aspect of the programme for improving the conditions of agricultural workers. It has been suggested that progress in the implementation of the minimum wage legislation should be reviewed from time to time at Inter-State Conferences, so that experience gained in meeting common problems may be pooled and the implementation of the legislation expedited.

Except Minimum Wages Act, 1948, only a few provisions of the above Acts are applicable to agricultural workers. Besides these, certain provision in other Acts, viz., (1) Contract Labour Act, 1970, (2) Equal Remuneration Act, 1976, (3) Inter State Migrant Workmen (Regulation of Employment and Conditions of Service) Act, 1979, and (4) Child Labour (Prohibition and Regulation) Act, 1986 give protection to the agricultural workers.

Inspite of all these Acts and Welfare Schemes the plight of agricultural labours is pitiful. The legislation, unless strongly backed by workers organisations on issue basis, is never enforced. In fact, Union Ministry of Labour while analysing the effectiveness of existing Acts and welfare schemes in its Annual Report for the year 1999-2000 pointed out that the existing Acts and welfare schemes have not adequately protected the interest of agricultural workers. The Ministry has envisaged alternative strategies such as creating 'Welfare Fund' by enacting yet another 'comprehensive' legislation for agricultural workers. Sadly, the preparation is continuing but it is never tabled in Parliament. An Agricultural Workers Bill was prepared in 1997 but kept in the files. The salient features of the pending Agricultural Workers' Bill are as follows:

- The definition of agricultural land is proposed to be kept sufficiently wide to cover all type of agricultural occupations and allied activities but excluding plantations as defined in the Plantation Labour Act, 1951.
- Provision for registration of agricultural workers and the landowners having one hectare or more of agricultural land and issue of identity cards to agricultural workers.
- Provisions of standard terms and conditions of employment such as hours of work, rest period, overtime, harvesting wages and for giving preference to employment to such workers as have worked on land in previous session.
- Provision for first-aid, shelter and other amenities.
- Appointment of conciliation officers for the redress of agricultural disputes.
- Provision for arbitration in the case of failure of conciliation at the local level.

- Creation of an Agricultural Workers Welfare Board and a welfare fund at the District level to be financed by employers' contribution on the basis of earnings from land and token voluntary contribution by workers. The fund will undertake various welfare/social security measures including financial assistance in case of death or injury/ payment of group insurance premium, health, maternity benefits, old age pension, housing and children's education etc.
- Provisions relating to penalties, monetary and imprisonment including trial of offences by Executive Magistrates and to exclude jurisdiction of Civil Courts.
- The State Government would be required under the proposed legislation to constitute District Level Welfare Boards, which will administer the fund. The cess is proposed to be collected by the State Revenue Machinery and the Boards would be permitted to incur upto 5 per cent of their expenditure on salaries and other administrative costs of the fund. The Welfare fund is proposed to be financed through:
  (a) Contributions made by landowners,
  (b) Any grants/loans by the Government,
  (c) Contributions made by beneficiaries,
  (d) Such other sources as may be decided by the Government.

The workers went on *dharna* in 1998 to pressurise the government to table the Bill. The then Cabinet Committee just passed the bill and nothing has happened since then. In 1999 another modified version of the bill was prepared and the story of negligence continues.

Bonded Labour System (Abolition) Act, 1976

It is an Act to provide for the abolition of bonded labour system with a view to preventing the economic and physical exploitation of the weaker sections of the people especially the agricultural labour. Some landless labours are bonded labours and this act is very much beneficial for them. Under this act "bonded labour" means any labour or service rendered under the bonded labour system and "bonded labour" means a labour who incurs, or has, or is presumed to have, incurred, a bonded debt. "bonded labour system" means the system of forced, or partly forced labour under which a debtor enters, or has, or is presumed to have, entered, into an agreement with the creditor to the effect that – (i) in consideration of an advance obtained by him or by any of his lineal ascendants or descendants (whether or not such advance is evidenced by the document) and in consideration of the interest, if any, due on such advance, or (ii) in pursuance of any customary or social obligation, or (iii) in pursuance of any obligation devolving on him by succession, or (iv) for any economic consideration received by him or by any of his lineal ascendants or descendants, or (v) by reason of his birth in any particular caste or community, he would — (1) render, by himself or through any member of his family, or any person dependent on him, labour or service, to the creditor, or for the benefit of the creditor, for a specific period or for an unspecified period, either without wages or for nominal wages, or (2) forfeit the freedom of employment or other means of livelihood for an specified period or for an unspecified period, or (3) forfeit the right to move freely throughout the territory of India, or (4) forfeit the right to appropriate or sell at market-value any of his property or product of his labour or the labour of a member of his family or any person dependent on him and includes the system of forced, or partly forced, labour under which a surety for a debtor enters, or has, or is presumed to have, entered into an agreement with the creditor to the effect that in the event of the failure of the debtor to repay the debt, he would render the bonded labour on behalf of the debtor. This system has made several agricultural labours slaves to some creditors.

On the commencement of this Act, the bonded labour system shall stand abolished and every bonded labour shall, on such commencement, stand freed and discharged from any obligation to render, any bonded labour. After the commencement of this Act, no person shall (a) make any advance under, or in pursuance of, the bonded labour system, or (b) compel any person to render any bonded labour or other form of forced labour. On the commencement of this Act, any custom or tradition or any contract, agreement or other instrument (whether entered into or executed before or after the commencement of this Act) by virtue of which any person, or any member of the family or dependent of such person, is required to do any work or render any service as a bonded labour, shall be void and inoperative. On the commencement of this Act, every obligation of a bonded labour to repay any bonded debt, or such part of any bonded debt unsatisfied immediately before such commencement, shall be deemed to have been extinguished. After the commencement of this Act, no suit or other proceedings shall lie in any civil or before any other authority for the recovery of any bonded debt or any part thereof. Every decree or order for the recovery of bonded debt, passed before the commencement of this Act and not fully satisfied before such commencement, shall be deemed, on such commencement, to have been fully satisfied. Every attachment made before the commencement of this Act, for the recovery of any bonded debt, shall, on such commencement, stand vacated; and where, in pursuance of such attachment, any movable property of the bonded labour was seized and removed from his custody and kept in the custody of any court or other authority pending sale thereof, such movable property shall be restored, as soon as may be practicable after such commencement, to the possession of the bonded labour. Where, before the commencement of this Act, possession of any property belonging to a bonded labour or a member of his family or other dependent was forcibly taken over by any creditor for the recovery of any bonded debt, such property shall be restored, as soon as may be practicable after such commencement, to the possession of the person from whom it was seized.

All property vested in a bonded labour which was immediately before the commencement of this Act under any mortgage, charge, lien or other encumbrances in connection with any bonded debt shall, in so far as it is relatable to the bonded debt, stand freed and discharged from such mortgage, charge, lien or other encumbrances, and where any such property was, immediately before the commencement of this Act, in the possession of the mortgage or the holder of the charge, lien or encumbrance, such property shall (except where it was subject to any other charges), on such commencement, be restored to the possession of the bonded labour. If any delay is made in restoring any property, referred to in sub-section (1), to the possession of the bonded labour, such labour shall be entitled, on and from the date of such commencement, to recover from the mortgage or holder of the lien, charge or encumbrance, such mesne profits as may be determined by the civil court of the lowest pecuniary jurisdiction within the local limits of whose jurisdiction such property is situated.

No person who has been freed and discharged under this Act from any obligation to render any bonded labour, shall be evicted from any homestead or other residential premises which he was occupying immediately before the commencement of this Act as part of the consideration for the bonded labour. If, after the commencement of this Act, any such person is evicted by the creditor from any homestead or other residential premises, referred to in sub-section (1), the Executive Magistrate in charge of the Sub-Division within which such homestead or residential premises is situated shall, as practicable, restore the bonded labour to the possession of such homestead or other residential premises.

No creditor shall accept any payment against any bonded debt which has been extinguished or deemed to have been extinguished or fully satisfied by virtue of the provisions of this Act. Whoever contravenes the provisions of sub-section (1), shall be punishable with imprisonment for a term which may extend to three years and also with fine. The court, convicting any person under sub-section (2) may, in addition to the penalties which may be imposed under that sub-section, direct the person to deposit, in court, the amount accepted in contravention of the provisions of sub-section (1), within such period as may be specified in the order for being refunded to the bonded labour.

Whoever enforces, after the commencement of this Act, any

custom, tradition, contract, agreement or other instrument, by virtue of which any person or any member of the family of such person or any dependent of such person is required to render any service under the bonded labour system, shall be punishable with imprisonment for a term which may extend to three years and also with fine which may extend to two thousand rupees; and, out of the fine, if recovered, payment shall be made to the bonded labour at the rate of rupees five for each day for which the bonded labour was extracted from him.

ILO Standards and International Conventions for Rural Workers

From the very start, the ILO has been concerned with the problems of rural workers, especially their right of association. Some of them are as follows:

- Right of Association (Agriculture) Convention (No.11).
- Right to Organise and Collective Bargaining Convention, (No. 98).
- The Rural Workers' Organisations Convention, 1975 (No. 141) gives a very clear definition of rural workers which encompasses both wage earning and self-employed, and includes the landless and other forms of employment in rural areas.
- Recommendation No. 149 describes in detail the role that should be played by Rural Workers' Organisations and recommends a number of means of encouraging the establishment and growth of such organisations, including legislative and administrative measures.

Charter of Demands

This Charter of Demands was adopted by more than 3000 landless delegates from communities across South Africa and their landless allies from across the world at the Landless People's Assembly held in Durban on 30 August, 2001 - the Day of the Landless at the 3rd United Nations World Conference against Racism—as an initiative of the Landless People's Movement. This campaign was organised by The Landless People's Movement (LPM), The National Land Committee (NLC), The Rural Development Services Network (RDSN) and The South African NGO Coalition (SANGOCO). On this conference the landless labours asserted their rights. Some relevant clauses are edited and presented here. The entire document is given in the annexure.

"We, the farm workers and labour tenants, demand access to land and security of tenure. Laws and practices which victimise us must be scrapped, and institutions which fail to serve our needs must be transformed" :

(1) Farm workers and labour tenants should be given land of their own.
(2) The government must declare a moratorium on all evictions until a new law is adopted to protect farm dwellers.
(3) Farm owners who abuse and exploit their workers must be prosecuted and must forfeit their land for land reform.
(4) We demand a halt to all evictions of labour tenants and farm workers. The Extension of Security of Tenure Act and the Land Reform (Labour Tenants) Act must be amended to stop evictions and give farm dweller real land rights. We want legal protection and security of tenure.
(5) We should not lose our homes if we do not continue working on the farm, or if we are disabled or pensioned. The wives and widows of farm workers must not be thrown off the land because of the circumstances of their husbands.
(6) Laws must be passed to protect people working on farms from abuse and exploitation. These laws must include minimum wages. Firm steps must be taken to oversee that labour laws on farms are implemented.
(7) Farm workers must be informed of their new rights, and provided with adequate legal support to enforce them. Farm workers should also be involved in making laws.

(8) Farm workers should be paid the same rates as other workers in towns because they work equally hard.

(9) Women farm workers should be paid the same as men.

(10) A fair share of the rural policing budget should be spent protecting our rights.

(11) Rural police, magistrates and prosecutors who fail to protect our rights must be fired and prosecuted.

(12) Farm workers and tenants must be given secure rights to plough and graze their cattle. These rights should be protected when a farm changes hands.

(13) Farmers must be responsible for supporting orphaned children of deceased workers.

(14) We want an end to child labour on farms. People breaking this law must be monitored and severely punished.

(15) Farm evictees, tenants and other landless people should be given top priority in any land reform programme.

(16) Groups who can serve and assist farm dwellers should immediately have free access to the farms. Farm worker unions should be legally entitled to organise workers on farms.

(17) Special pieces of land should be set aside for farm workers villages.

(18) We must be able to bury our loved ones on the farms where we live.

(19) The government should take ownership of portions of land on farms for the use of the people living on the farms. This land can be used for schools, sports fields and clinics, for example, which must be owned and run by the state instead of the farmers.

(20) Farm workers must be provided with safe transportation to and from towns.

(21) Farmers must not be allowed to employ immigrant workers on three-month contracts, and the rights of immigrant workers should be protected to prevent use of immigrant labour from undermining farm workers' rights and wage levels.

Women: "Women must be able to own land, and have equal rights in all areas of their lives".

(1) Women should be able to own land whether they are married or single. Women and men should have the same rights to land. Married couples should have their houses registered in the names of both spouses.
(2) Women should have equal representation on local government and other decision-making structures affecting their lives, including traditional authorities.
(3) There should be no discrimination against women in inheritance rights.
(4) Women should benefit from development programmes and be targeted for training. There should be special training centres and adult education courses geared for women.
(5) Women living on farms must have secure places to live.
(6) There should be special housing subsidies for women who cannot afford to buy houses or pay rent. Housing subsidies must be introduced to assist women who are single parents.
(7) Land should be set aside for community facilities that benefit women, such as crèches, community gardens and women's training centres.
(8) Women and children must have places to go if they are abused.
(9) Rural development plans, especially job creation and skills development programmes, must prioritise the needs of women and must include adequate means of monitoring their actual impact on women.
(10) The quota system of affirmative action should be imposed in tribal authorities and other rural structures, and tribal laws and practice that oppress rural women should be reviewed.

THE WAY FORWARD: "Landless people must organise or starve" We must form local structures in all our communities to take forward our demands.

We, as the landless women of South Africa, must build women's forums in our regions to discuss land, and organise ourselves at a local and regional level to make sure our concerns are addressed.

We must build solidarity with other landless people throughout the world.

We must send a memorandum from this conference to the present government to make sure they know what our demands are.

We must organise local and regional actions to support our demands.

If our demands are not met, we will launch a campaign to occupy vacant land and state land, and return to our land.

These demands we will fight for, side by side throughout our lives, until we have won our land (www.un.org).

Even if this charter of rights of the landless labours is formulated in South Africa, this declaration reflects the mind of landless women labour worldwide. This declaration gives flesh and blood to the aspiration of landless women labours. It shows clearly that the problems of landless women labours are similar in different parts of the world. In India, the situation is not better. If apartheid is the issue which affect adversely the landless labours in South Africa, it is the caste based discrimination that adds to the miseries of landless labours in India.

Concluding Remarks

It is understood that women are responsible for producing food. They have least access to means of production, receive lowest wages and know least about how to protect them from exploitation impended upon them. There exists hardly any policy or legal provision especially meant for them, and if there is any they are not aware of it. Gender based division of labour gives a very clear reflection of gender-based technology. Migration of rural men to urban areas in search of better employment opportunities has increased the number of women who have to carry the full burden of earning income and managing household for their families. Being a woman and poor landless labour, she is highly vulnerable to all kind of harassment–physical, economical and sexual harassment.

There are numerous problems for women in agriculture, especially landless labour. The solution to all these problems requires affirmative action on the part of policy-makers within government, international agencies and non-governmental organisations. There is a strong need to protect their right to have access to land, to protect them from all kind of harassment. It is very important for women empowerment. Recognising women's worth as economic producer is not only imperative for gender equality, but also to achieve larger objectives of higher economic growth, poverty alleviation, and human development.

Chapter 4

RESEARCH METHODOLOGY

This research proposal addresses the issues of landless unorganised female labour force. Landless unorganised female labour force is probably the most miserable section of the society. They work on the farms of others during season. Rest of the time, they remain unemployed. They form highly marginalised and extremely deprived group which is excluded from the mainstream society. When we study the ratio of unorganised labour we see that in India 97 per cent labour force is unorganised. According to the statistics only 4.2 per cent women work in organised sectors. Rest of them (95.8 %) are unorganised. The distribution of female work participation by status of employment as the NSSO 50th round (1993-94) shows that 57 per cent of women in rural areas are self employed, 2.1 per cent are regular employees and 40.9 per cent are working as casual labours. They keep on changing their occupations but most of the time they work as landless labours (NSSO, 1994).

This is indeed the group, which is not only highly impoverished section of the society but also represents feminisation of poverty. Landless labours, especially women, are involved in most precarious and least rewarding work. This is an extremely poor group, which is not sure of the next meal. Nearly 1.3 billion people all over the world are suffering from persistent hunger and poverty. Strangely enough 70 per cent of them are women. Landless agriculture women work forms a section of extremely poor group. As payment to women worker is less than the wages of their male counterparts, usually they are at the bottom as far as economic status is concerned. Here it is significant to note that there are other section of women who are equally or more miserable but this section projects an image of rural masses who suffer from all kinds of deprivations.

Despite the fact that these women agricultural workers comprises more than 70 million women all over India, they are highly marginalised. Wage structure for them is highly discriminatory. Not only this, they often suffer from work place harassment as well.

Their problems are compounded by the fact that they are neglected in all welfare and developmental programmes meant specifically for women. They are unidentified and "invisible" inspite of being a big group. Also, they cannot get any protection of legal provisions, as they are not a part of organised labour.

Thus, they are poor, illiterate, undernourished, socially excluded and grossly exploited section. Due to illiteracy and lack of awareness they have no knowledge of their 'welfare rights'. Their poverty, lower status and deprivation are transferred to the next generation as a natural flow of events. More deprived among them are the Schedule Castes, Scheduled Tribes and minorities as they are poorest of the poor.

It is against this backdrop that the given proposal will study the magnitude and intensity of their problems these women workers are facing and specific problems of the minorities and SC and ST groups among them. It will further study their desires, visions and aspirations for themselves and for their children.

Any endeavour towards intervening for improving their lot requires examining the role of various socio-political institutions in their lives and the impact of governmental and non-governmental welfare activities if any, on the studied group. The study would thus explore new and evolving needs of these women workers in this direction. Besides, it will try to suggest some measures, which can bring about some improvement in their life style, mental make up and socio economic situation.

This study uncovers the image of rural women who suffer from different kinds of deprivation. Salient features of this group are the following:

- This is a large group of people comprising more than 70 million women all over India.

- This group of landless women labour is the most disadvantaged and deprived group as they hardly have access to health services, education, recreation and other forms of development. They are poor, illiterate, under-nourished, socially excluded and grossly exploited section of the society.
- From the point of view of human poverty they are the most vulnerable section. They are at the bottom of human poverty line.
- Their poverty, lower status and deprivation are transferred to the succeeding generations in a hereditary manner.
- These women have a very low self-image; their awareness level is also considerably low. They are not aware of the empowerment policy launched by the Government in the year 2001.
- All the welfare and developmental programmes for women ignore this section. It is seen at the completion of IX plan that their economic standard, quality of life and life style have not changed.
- More deprived among them are schedule castes, schedule tribes and minorities.
- Landless women labours cannot get any protection of legal provisions, as they are not a part of organised labour. They are unidentified and invisible inspite of being a big group. Due to the invisibility, they cannot get the advantage of legal protective shields.

Keeping the status of landless women labours in mind, a detailed study was planned.

Rationale and the Need of Study

It has already been mentioned that this section is highly deprived. There are some other points, which indicate the need and urgency of this study.

- These landless labour women are quite often half fed and remain most vulnerable.

- Wage structure for them is highly discriminatory.
- Quite often they suffer from workplace harassment.
- They keep on working in fields and the eldest girl child remains deprived of education and recreation and marches into adulthood without enjoying his/her childhood.
- Technological advancement affects adversely on them. In other words their situation become more depressed with social and economic development and market friendly economy.
- Due to illiteracy and lack of awareness they have no knowledge of their rights. As a result of this ignorance government machinery ignores them.

Research Design

The research is a descriptive study, using sample survey design. The problems of landless women labour are described in the study, suggesting some useful measures to improve the situation. While describing the general problems of landless women labours, special attention is given to narrate their empowerment problems.

Universe and Sampling

The universe of the study consists of landless women labours from the States of Delhi, U.P. and Haryana. Since no reports are available about the exact number of landless women workers in these states, the universe remain unestimated. The sample consists of 750 respondents belonging to five agriculture dominated districts of the concerned states consisting of 250 respondents from each of the states.

Objectives of the Study

To understand the magnitude and intensity of the problem concerning landless labour women in the states of Delhi, U.P. and Haryana.

To study the respondents' desires, vision and aspirations for themselves and for their children.

- To find out the impact of governmental and non-governmental welfare activities if any on the landless women labours.
- To examine the role of various socio-political institutions in their lives.
- To analyse the specific problems of SC and ST group of women who are working as landless labours.
- To suggest some measures which can bring about some improvement in their life style, self-profile and socio-economic situation.

Research Tools

For data collection the following tools will be used:

- Interview schedules for landless labour women were the major instruments for primary data collection. This interview schedule contained queries about the following:
- General socio-economic status.
- Occupational and economic status.
- Problems specific of the landless women labours.
- Effectiveness of Governmental and Non-governmental schemes.

Other tools of the research include,

- Observation sheet for recording investigator's remarks.
- Interview guide for government officers and NGOs functionaries.
- Focussed group discussion, at least one in every village.
- Benchmark data like reports, government records, rescarch and evaluation report etc.

Data Analysis

Statistical Package for Social Sciences (SPSS) is the software used for data analysis and presentation. Data collected were classified, tabulated and presented. At the primary analysis, diagrammatic presentation, one way and two-way tables and derivation of central tendencies such as mean and standard deviation are found out. At the secondary analysis tests of significance and correlation analysis are conducted.

While preparing the research report, the content were divided in to nine chapters excluding the annexure. The first four chapters were for the theoretical analysis of the theme and for the presentation of secondary data. The next four chapters included the finding of the research or the primary data. Last chapter consists of the summary statement and conclusion of the study. Some useful reading materials including the copy of the interview schedule used for the study are given in the annexure. The reading materials include the U.N. document on the rights of landless women labour and various legislations affecting the landless women labour.

Operational Definitions

The important terms to be defined are the 'victims of social injustice' and 'landless women labour'. These terms are used in their wider sense in the context of the present research.

Victims of Social Injustice

Victims of social injustice refer to those people who are victimised by the conscious or unintentional acts of the government. The victims of injustice often remain invisible in the social field. To cite an example, we take the case of reservation for women in professional courses or reservation in government jobs. While 85 per cent of the landless women labour remain illiterate, what impact would these measures bring in their lives? Many of the landless women labour do not have access to various welfare schemes of the government due to their enforced inability. Provisions of maternity leave, minimum wages, workmen's compensation, provident fund and ESI benefits are applicable only to employees of industrial sectors or of notified plantations. Therefore, majority of landless women labour are systematically kept away from the access to these labour welfare measures. The provisions of industrial dispute acts are not applicable to this invisible group of landless women labour.

Educational and literacy programmes are accessible only to those women who have leisure the working class women seldom get chance to attend adult educational programmes. These women who are systematically marginalised are called the victims of social injustice. In the eyes of the policy-makers, justice is being done against the offenders of the law and the victims of injustice are often ignored and neglected by them. It is high time for the responsible hands to listen to the problems of the victims of social injustice.

Landless Women Labour

Landless women labour in the context of the research refer to those women who do not have agricultural land of their own but engage themselves as casual labours in agricultural operations in others' fields. Since the agricultural operations in the States of U.P., Haryana and Delhi are seasonal, the landless women labour are under employed or unemployed for non-agricultural seasons. During this time most of them engage themselves as construction workers. Since the landless women labour are never engaged as regular employees anywhere and they are deprived of any benefits prescribed under labour laws. This is the special feature of landless women labour and little attention is given to the problems of these women by both governmental and non-governmental agencies to the specific problems of this section of the society.

Chapter 5

DEMOGRAPHIC AND SOCIAL PROFILE OF LANDLESS WOMEN LABOUR

Social background of the respondents is described in this chapter. Social profile of the respondents includes age, marital status, place of origin, place of destination, caste, head of household, age of the husband, age of the head of the household, sex of the head of the household, education level of the respondent, education level of the husband, education level of the head of the household, education level of the most educated member in the family, desire of the respondents to study, type of family, size of family, opinion of the respondents about marriage, future plans for sons and daughters, interest in village level politics as well as the level of interest in it. Social and educational status of the respondents can be estimated clearly from the tables presented in this chapter. It is seen that the social and educational status of landless women labour (LWL) is rather better in Delhi compared to the same in the neighbouring States of U.P. and Haryana.

Understanding the social and educational profile of the respondents is an important aspect of estimating the magnitude of injustice faced by the respondents in social, economic, educational and occupational fields of life. The specific problems of landless women labour (LWL) are to be analysed keeping in mind their unique socio-economic background. Understanding the demographic and social profile of the respondents is useful to find out the present status from which they aspire for a better future. This understanding helps us to locate the community of landless women labour (LWL) in their right place in the larger context of our developing nation.

The information regarding their social background helps us to compare their social status with that of the national status and various other marginalised women of India. Demographic and social factors serve as the independent variables to analyse the magnitude of various problems faced by LWL. Demographic and social profile of the respondents can be analysed under various categories, such as demographic profile, educational profile and socio-cultural profile.

Demographic Profile of the Respondents

Demographic profile of the respondents include, age, marital status, place of origin, place of destination, caste, head of household, age of the husband, age of the head of the household and sex of the head of the household. Demographic details constitute the basic socio-economic data by which we understand the bio-statistics of the respondents. This basic data gives us the starting point of understanding the respondents. These details furnish the basic frame of reference regarding the physiological and geographical status of the respondents. This data is very important to formulate the first impression about the respondents. Understanding of the demographic profile of the respondents is very important to measure the right magnitude of social injustice they face.

Table 5.1 : Age of the respondents.

Age of the respondent (years)	*Frequency*	*(%)*
20–25	247	32.9
26–30	118	15.7
31–35	138	18.4
36–40	45	6.0
41–45	68	9.1
46–50	26	3.5
51 or more	108	14.4
Total	**750**	**100.0**

It can be seen from the Table 5.1 that nearly 33 per cent of the respondents are below 25 years of age while 48 per cent of the respondents are below 30 years of age. Several reasons account for this finding. It can be inferred that agricultural works are labour intensive and young and healthy persons will only succeed in these unskilled tasks. Older persons can't undertake such works for long hours. Since agricultural job does not require any special skill or educational qualifications, women enter into agricultural works at an early age leaving their schooling and remain life long in this occupation. Agricultural works go along with fuel gathering, cattle rearing, and other domestic chores like cooking, cleaning and washing. With all these works they remain very busy all the day long.

Table 5.2 : Marital Status of the respondents.

Age of the respondent (in years)	*Marital status*			*Total*
	Single	*Married*	*Widow*	
20–25	44	203		247
26–30		118		118
31–35		138		138
36–40		43	2	45
41–45		58	10	68
46–50		19	7	26
51 or more		41	67	108
Total	**44**	**620**	**86**	**750**

As many as 83 per cent of the respondents are married and 6 per cent of the respondents are unmarried. Most of the respondents get married at their twenties and many of them become widows in their fifties. We see none remain unmarried after the age of 25. Early marriage of women is one thing very much encouraged in the rural areas. In Delhi, which is more urbanised than U.P. and Haryana, the age of marriage for women is higher. Therefore, we find more single women in Delhi. Widows are 11 per cent. Among the 108 landless women labour who are above the age of 50, 67 are widows. It confirms the general findings that women survive their spouses and there are more widows than widowers. Since men prefer to marry younger women there is naturally a greater chance for women to survive their men. The traditional factors also contribute to this situation. Remarriage of widower is easier than remarriage of widows in India. Because of all these factors, there are more women without spouses than those with spouses in the age group of 50 and above. The pressure for working is more in the case of widows and the separated women.

Table 5.3 : Place of origin and destination of the respondents.

Place of origin	*Place of Destination*			*Total*
	Delhi	*U.P.*	*Haryana*	
Delhi	28	19	26	73
U.P.	214	191	206	611
Bihar	1	5	1	7
Haryana		7	1	8
NADK	7	31	13	51
Total	**250**	**253**	**247**	**750**

We see from the Table 5.3 that majority of the respondents are from the State of U.P. From the State of Haryana there are very few landless women labour, so too from the State of Bihar. Out of the 247 respondents who belong to Haryana, 206 come from the state of U.P. Similarly out of 250 respondents from the State of Delhi, 214 are migrants from U.P.

Haryana being the richest state in terms of agricultural production, has attracted landless women labour from the State of U.P. Landlessness is a rare phenomenon in the state of Haryana. It is very common in the State of U.P. Uttar Pradesh is the poorest amongst three states under the investigation. Natural resources are also comparatively less in U.P. Most of the agricultural regions are draught prone and both rain and river water resources are scarce. In terms of literacy and employment too the State of Uttar Pradesh is at the lowest among the three. Landless women and men migrate to the neighbouring states looking for a livelihood. That is why we have found more landless women labourfolk originally belong to the State of Uttar Pradesh.

Even if there are many migrants from the State of Bihar in Delhi, U.P. and Haryana, it is seen from the table that migrants from Bihar do not fall under the category of landless women labour, or many such women do not disclose their identity.

Table 5.4 : Religion.

Religion	*Frequency*	*(%)*
Hindu	653	87.1
Muslim	67	8.9
Sikh	30	4.0
Total	**750**	**100.0**

It is seen from the Table 5.4 that majority of the respondents are Hindus by religion. Hindus, especially those who belong to the scheduled and the backward caste are bound to agriculture and allied occupation while the other religious groups in India are more engaged in non-agricultural occupations.

It is the general fact that Muslims are less tied to agricultural occupations. The Sikhs are agricultural communities but they are concentrated in the State of Punjab. Therefore, it is found that there are very few of them got included in the sample of the study.

More than 87 per cent of the respondents are Hindus. Many a landless households are the scheduled castes. They were in fact the landlords prior to the arrival of the British or even the Mughals. The sons of the soil were deprived of their ownership due to several reasons that are historical. Since majority of them were illiterate, they hardly knew the importance of acquisition of land rights. They kept or working in some plots of land offering the fruits of their labour to 'some lords' at every point of history. Prior to the arrival of the Muslims, these people offered their produce to the Rajas who were subsequently substituted by the Sultans and finally the colonial powers. Only in the independent India, they have realised the problem of landlessness and deprivations. The higher caste groups with better educational background could easily establish their right of ownership over agricultural land where the Dalits and the scheduled caste groups were traditionally working.

Table 5.5 : Caste

Caste	*Frequency*	*Per cent*
UC	6	0.8
BC	226	30.1
SC	316	42.1
ST	158	21.1
NADK	44	5.9
Total	**750**	**100.0**

We see from the above Table 5.5 that only 6 respondents belong to the upper caste and more than 90 per cent of the landless women labour belong to the backward/scheduled cast and the scheduled tribes. The issue of caste is not applicable to Sikh and the Muslims, hence 5 per cent of the respondents who belong to Sikhs or Muslim religion did not respond to this query.

What is emphasised by this finding is that agricultural operations which are the basic and primary economic activities, the least skilled, the least remunerative were assigned to the backward and the scheduled caste population. Land-holding was traditionally the right of the higher castes and the labourers were of the lower castes. The remuneration for the landless labourers was mostly in kind. Bonded labour is very much common among the landless labourers.

Educational status of landless labourers is relatively low and the educated ones rarely stick to agricultural occupations. It is well established fact that the scheduled caste and the scheduled tribes except the people of North Eastern States are the least educated, least skilled and the least qualified workforce. Not only that the scheduled caste groups stick on agricultural works, they put great value in this work. They consider land as an object of worship. Working in the agricultural land was always preferred. Therefore, offer of alternative occupations in terms of cottage industries and small scale industries did not attract them.

The Table 5.6 clearly shows that most of the respondents have their husbands more aged than themselves. Only two women are

Table 5.6 : Age of the husband

Age of the husband (years)	*Age of the respondent (years)*							*Total*
	20-25	*26-30*	*31-35*	*36-40*	*41-45*	*46-50*	*51 or more*	
20-25	67							67
26-30	115	48						163
31-35	19	60	28	1				108
36-40	2	8	101	20			1	132
41-45	2		7	16	18			43
46-50			2	3	36	6		47
51 or more		2		3	4	16	43	68
NADK	42			2	10	4	64	122
Total	**247**	**118**	**138**	**45**	**68**	**26**	**108**	**750**

married to men of younger age. 122 respondents are either unmarried or are widows, hence they did not respond to this query. The age difference between the couples is on an average of 5 to 10 years. This age difference at the time of marriage was very much accepted in traditional rural communities.

Girls attain puberty at the age of 13 or 14 and are considered eligible for marriage by traditional societies both in India and outside India; while boys attain puberty only after the age of 15 or 16. This natural gaining of sexual maturity by the girls ahead of boys contributes to the tendency of early marriages of girls compared to the boys of the similar age.

Another reason for the age difference between husbands and wives is that the Indian society is patriarchal and in the patriarchal families the men are the heads of the family. It is easier for an elder husband to exercise control upon a younger wife. Therefore, men prefer to marry younger women with the intention of keeping them always under their patriarchal control.

It can be seen from the Table 5.7 that nearly 90 per cent of the households are headed by men. Four households where women are the heads, the husbands are of younger age. Such incidence is rare and hence insignificant. Out of the 80 households headed by women, 76 are widows. This finding confirms the fact that Indian

Table 5.7 : Sex of the head of the household.

Marital status of LWL	*Sex of the head of household*		*Total*
Male	*Female*		
Single	44		44
Married	616	4	620
Widow	10	76	86
Total	**670**	**80**	**750**

society is patriarchal and Indian women accept unconditionally the authority of their husbands or fathers at home. Women head the household only in such a situation where they find no male members at home to be pointed out as the head of the household.

Educational and Social Profile

Educational and social profile of the respondents refers to education level of the respondent, education level of the husband, education level of the head of the household, education level of the most educated member in the family, the respondents' desire to study, type of family, size of family, opinion of the respondents about marriage, future plans for sons, future plans for daughters, interest of the respondents in village level politics, level of interest in village level politics etc. These data helps us to understand the essential social and educational status of the landless women labour in comparison to the national scenario.

During the study it is found that the majority of the respondents are socially and educationally the most backward sections of the society. Their social and educational status is much below the national average.

It is seen from the Table 5.8 that about 85 per cent of the respondents are illiterate. Literacy rate of the landless women labour is nowhere near to the national average. This explains the susceptibility of this vulnerable section of population to easy exploitation. This confirms the general belief that the victims of social justice are the least educated, the marginalised and the most backward section of the society. Only 15 per cent of the respondents

Table 5.8 : Education level of the respondent.

Age of the respondent (years)	*Education of the respondent*			*Total*
	Illiterate	*Upto primary*	*NADK*	
20-25	184	63		247
26-30	100	18		118
31-35	115	22	1	138
36-40	39	6		45
41-45	63	5		68
46-50	26			26
51 or more	106		2	108
Total	**633**	**114**	**3**	**750**

have reached up to their primary level of education. We can also see that the respondents who are literate are of younger age. It sets the progressive trend. The younger generation is better educated.

This Table also illustrates the fact that agricultural work is mainly an unskilled job and educational qualification is not a relevant factor for entering in to this occupation. Those who have reached the primary level of education could not continue their studies after primary education, either due to financial difficulties, or due to marriage or due to gender bias of the parents.

There is another reason for this finding. Education is also seen as a liberative factor. While selecting the samples for the study the primary criterion considered was whether there were any women presently working as landless labourers or not. The study does not include the families who were once households of landless women labourers. It is quite possible that some landless women labour who were educated and employed in non agricultural occupations are left out from the study. Women with higher education do not prefer to remain as agricultural labour.

Table 5.9 reveals that 50 per cent of the respondents have their husband who are also illiterate. At least 35 per cent of the respondents who are illiterate have their husbands literate. The overall observation from the Table shows that the educational status of landless men labourer is definitely higher than that of women. Literacy level of the husbands is 50 per cent while that of wives is

Table 5.9 : Education level of the husband.

Education of the husband	*Education of the respondent*			*Total*
	Illiterate	*Upto primary*	*NADK*	
Illiterate	370			370
Upto primary	60	32	1	93
Upto middle	102	51		153
Upto secondary	17			17
NADK	84	31	2	117
Total	**633**	**114**	**3**	**750**

only 15 per cent. This reveals that the parents prefer to educate the boy children and send the girls for work in the field.

The illiterate women seldom resist injustice done against them. They are easily kept under fear of dismissal at the workplace. They are afraid to react against harassment. They get easily subjugated by physical threat. They tend to respect the customs and traditions. Anything in the name of religion, faith and superstitious beliefs would appeal them and bring their obedience. They are rather afraid to approach the police and the court. Illiteracy is the first social evil to be eradicated from the masses. Education opens up ways and means to protect justice. Unless the landless women labour are made literate, no reforms both political and legal would bring out any desirable result.

Educational status of the best educated member of the family Table 5.10 shows the upward trend in the social status of the families of the respondents. Better educated members in the family would lead the entire household to economic prosperity and social advancement. Better educated members in the family facilitate better education of the future generations. Higher level of education gives opportunities for more choices in the occupational scenario. The better educated members of the family get better jobs and get settled in life easier than the illiterate members of the family.

We can see from the Table 5.10 that most of the families have literate family members. 274 respondents who have not responded to this query do not have any other family members who are more

Table 5.10 : Education level of the most educated member in the family.

Education of the most educated member in family	*Education of the respondent* *Illiterate*	*Upto primary*	*NADK*	*Total*
Just literate	4			4
Upto primary	125	50		175
Upto middle	178	58	1	237
Upto secondary	52	6	2	60
NADK	274			274
Total	**633**	**114**	**3**	**750**

educated than themselves. These respondents are illiterate. Thus it is seen that at least one third of the families are totally illiterate. The parents who are illiterate do not realise the need for educating their children; hence the respondents whose parents are illiterate tend to remain illiterate as in the case of 274 respondents.

It can also be seen that educational status of the respondents is higher in the families with better educated members. Education is however not regarded as a significant matter by the respondents. The impact of education upon the social status of the respondents is often invisible. Therefore, considerable efforts are required to make the illiterate landless households literate.

Table 5.11 : The want to study.

Do you want to study	*Frequency*	*(%)*
Yes	87	11.6
Not sure	21	2.8
No	379	50.5
Never thought of it	105	14.1
Any other	1	0.1
NADK	157	20.9
Total	**750**	**100.0**

Desire to study is an upward trend in the social status of the family. Education is the stepping stone to better occupation. Career oriented women express their wish to study higher. One of the primary objectives of education is to enkindle the aspiration for higher studies. It is also possible that the illiterate and the poor people seldom realise the importance of education. Therefore, child marriage and child labour are very common among the poorest of the poor families who are illiterate. Since the landless women labourers are too poor to invest any means for the education of the children, they employ them in the fields and or at home. Education is just another head of unwanted expenditure for the poor. Therefore, we see from the Table 5.11 that only 11.6 per cent of the respondents have expressed their desire to study. 50 per cent of the respondents have told that they do not wish to continue study. Over 20 per cent of the respondents remained silent. 14 per cent of the respondents never thought of it.

Only a minority have openly expressed their desire to study. It may be due to the thought of over burden. Most of the respondents are undertaking the household duties other than the outside work. Studying either in literacy classes or under regular stream would add to the burden the respondents already have. When they told that they don't want to study, they really meant that they do not want to take up additional burden in their busy life schedule.

Table 5.12 : Type of family.

Family members actual	*Type of family*			*Total*
	Nuclear	*Joint*	*Broken*	
Less than 3 members	195	6	3	204
Between 4 to 6 members	322	59		381
7 or above	66	99		165
Total	**583**	**164**	**3**	**750**

It is seen from the Table 5.12 that most of the families of the respondents are nuclear families. Most of the families are of medium size with 4 – 6 members. Nearly one third of the families are large families with more than 7 members. Joint families are mostly large size. Out of the 164 joint families only 6 families are small size families. Average number of members per family is five. Family size is a significant variable with regard to the economic status of the family. Families with large number of people have less per capita income and they tend to remain poor. Illiterate parents refrain from adopting any family planning methods and they consider that bigger families are better for greater economic security. They do not wish to teach their children.

It is generally found that the poor households are large sized. Illiteracy and poverty account for the large size of the families. Traditional and religious factors also contribute. Poor and superstitious mothers consider the children as divine blessings and regard family planning methods as against nature and the divine will. Their economic necessity compels them to employ the children especially the girl children instead of educating them for a bright future. There were some practical reasons for the women for not educating the girl children. Educated girls tend to incur more expenditure at the time of marriage and sometimes it seems very difficult to find out suitable match for an educated girl. It is much easier to find a match for an illiterate girl. Therefore, illiteracy and poverty affect the girl children most adversely.

Table 5.13 : Opinion of the unmarried respondents about marriage.

Think about marriage	*Frequency*	*(%)*
Want to be a housewife not a landless labour	11	1.5
Want a permanent job	6	0.8
Want to save my income	2	0.3
Want to remain what I am	17	2.3
Never thought of it	29	3.9
Any other	6	0.8
NADK	679	90.4
Total	**750**	**100.0**

Marriage is the most significant event in the life of men and women. People tend to have dreams and aspiration regarding this life changing event. The expectation regarding marriage is high among the educated people. It is seen that many illiterate women find marriage as a natural event in their life rather than something imposed by their parents. The poor and the illiterate women seldom exercise any right of choice with regard to their partners in marriage. The economic and social dependence of girl children upon their parents keep them under effective control. Therefore, the parental decision upon the marriage of their girl children is respected. The illiterate women seldom think seriously about their marriage and they prepare themselves to settle with whatever stuff comes in marriage and thereafter. They just try to adjust their life with any men who appear in the status of their husbands.

We see from the Table 5.13 that 90 per cent of the respondents have not responded because they were married and this query was not relevant to them. 3.9 per cent of the respondents have never thought of it. 2.3 per cent of the respondents seem to have the opinion not to get married as if they are being compelled to marry against their wish. 1.5 per cent of the respondents wish to live as housewives instead of remaining landless labour. It shows the wish of illiterate women to settle peacefully in life as housewives. Very few respondents are interested in securing a permanent job or saving money before getting married. Only a few unmarried respondents have realised the importance of economic independence before getting married.

Table 5.14 : Future plans for sons.

Future plans for sons	*Frequency*	*Per cent*
Study well and get good jobs	120	16.0
Study and be self-employed	194	25.9
Buy land and work on it	57	7.6
Get better wages	124	16.5
Never thought of it	138	18.4
Everything is decided by God	39	5.2
Any other	4	0.5
NADK	74	9.9
Total	**750**	**100.0**

The constantly reinforced patriarchal values at home make the parents to nurture high aspiration for their sons and low aspiration for the girl children. The parents weave great plans for their sons and poor career plans for the girl children. The parents expect their son to study well, get good jobs, earn higher wages, buy land and become rich while they expect their daughters to get married to a good family and nothing more. This discrimination in the future plans for the sons and daughters is very much reflected in the treatment given to them at home. When girl children are taught in cooking and housekeeping boy children are sent to school and given freedom to go out in pursuit of industrial jobs.

We see from the Table 5.14 that over 40 per cent of the respondents wish to educate their boys and prepare them for an alternate occupation. 25 per cent of the respondents wish their children to be self-employed. 16.5 per cent of the respondents wish that their children would get a better wage, while 7.6 per cent of the respondents wish to purchase land work and see that their children would work on that land. At least 23 per cent of the respondents have never thought of the future of their sons or have left the same in the hands of God. Overall observation shows that the aspiration of the parents regarding the future of the sons remains rather high.

Table 5.15 : Future plans for daughters.

Future plans for daughters	*Frequency*	*(%)*
Study and find career	23	3.1
Study and get married	106	14.1
Married as soon as possible	236	31.5
Never thought of it	145	19.3
Everything is decided by God	85	11.3
NADK	155	20.7
Total	**750**	**100.0**

This Table 5.15 describes the aspiration of the respondents regarding the future of their girl children. 20.7 per cent of the respondents do not have girl children, hence did not respond to this query. 31.5 per cent of the respondents have placed the highest priority on the marriage of their girl children. It seems that the most important concern for landless women labour is to get settled in marriage. Over 30 per cent of the respondents have either never thought of it or left to the decision by God. Barely 17 per cent of the respondents wish their girl children to study and 3 per cent of the respondents are concerned about the career of the girls. This finding is to be compared with the previous finding where over 40 per cent of the respondents have expressed their wish to educate their sons to secure an alternate career.

The difference in the aspirations regarding the future plan for sons and daughters shows the gender discrimination practised in the families of landless women labour. When their sons are oriented for a career in life, their daughters are oriented towards marriage. Gender discrimination is very much practised in the houses of the poorest of the poor, the illiterate and the marginalised. The aspiration about the future of the children is the basis of the treatment given to the children at home. When the boys are given freedom and opportunity to study, the girls are forced to practise household duties at the expense of learning.

Table 5.16 : Interest in village level politics.

Have you been interested in village level politics	*Frequency*	*(%)*
Yes	597	79.6
Not sure	6	0.8
No	139	18.5
NADK	8	1.1
Total	**750**	**100.0**

We see from the table 5.16 that majority of the respondents are politically active. Almost 80 per cent of the respondents are interested in village level politics. This is very encouraging phenomenon. The working class men as well as women were always the target group of various political parties, as they are important for the financial security of the party. Unionism is very much common among agricultural labourers as in the case of industrial workers. Only the domestic workers are relatively inactive as far as political activism is concerned. Land reforms are one of the important agenda for various regional and national political parties. The interest of political parties is limited in securing the vote of the landless labourers who are mostly illiterate. They seldom show interest in educating or improving the status of landless women labour.

Table 5.17 : Level of interest in village level politics.

Level of interest	*Frequency*	*(%)*
Voted	462	61.6
Voted and did canvassing	144	19.2
Contested also	3	0.4
Any other	2	0.3
NADK	139	18.5
Total	**750**	**100.0**

Almost 80 per cent of the respondents have participated in the village level politics at various levels. 3 respondents have contested the election. 18.5 per cent of the respondents who have not responded are not interested in the local level politics. 19.2 per cent of the respondents have participated in political canvassing while as many as 80 per cent of the respondents have voted. This is very high compared to the national average of 55 to 60 per cent. The participation of landless women labour in village level politics is not very much significant with regard to the impact they make in the political decision-making. The literacy rate of the respondents is as low as 15 per cent and their participation in political decision-making is very much limited. Their participation ends with voting or canvassing. Their problems are never taken up by any political parties and their issues are hardly taken care of by any legislatures in India. Therefore, we lack an effective legislation to protect the rights of landless women labour. They still remain largely illiterate and marginalised.

Concluding Remarks

Social and demographic profile of the respondents is described in this chapter. Majority of the respondents are below 35 years of age. Most of the respondents are married. None remain unmarried after the age of 25. Early marriage of women is one thing very much encouraged in the rural areas. There are more women without spouses than those with spouses in the age group of 50 and above. Since men prefer to marry younger women there is naturally a greater chance for women to survive their men. The age difference between the couples is on an average of 5 to 10 years. Most of the households are headed by men. Women head the household only in such a situation where they find no male members at home to be pointed out as the head of the household. Majority of the respondents are from the State of U.P. A vast majority of the landless women labour belong to the backward or scheduled caste and the scheduled tribes. Land-holding was traditionally the right of the higher castes and the labourers were of the lower castes. Majority of the respondents are illiterate. The younger generation is better educated. Parents prefer to educate the boy children and send the girls for work in the field. Most important concern for landless women labour is to get settled in marriage. Most of the respondents are undertaking the household duties other than the outside work. Most of the families of the respondents are nuclear families. Most of the families are medium size with 4 – 6 members. Average number of members per family is five. Majority of the respondents have shown their political interest by casting their vote.

Chapter 6

ECONOMIC AND OCCUPATIONAL PROFILE OF LANDLESS WOMEN LABOUR

Economic and occupational profile of landless women labour refers to occupation of the respondents, income of the respondents, occupation of the head of the household, income of the family, actual income, per capita income, land owned, working conditions, work on land, period of employment, other activities of the LWL, kind of their work, involvement in household activities, expenditure of the respondents and what their husbands do with their income.

Economically the landless women labour remain at the bottom of the rural communities. Both the husbands and the wives belong to working class in agricultural families. Here the work of women is not the sign of their empowerment, but a whole hearted attempt to survive. It is seen from a previous section that many respondents aspire to remain as housewives and wish their daughters to get settled down as housewives. When the illiterate women venture out to work, they face several hardships and harassment. The following tables show the economic and occupational profile of the respondents.

Economic Profile

Economic profile of the respondents shows that majority of the respondents belong to lower middle class group. Since they are unable to earn enough from their agricultural works, they do look for alternate and part-time occupations. Even the agricultural operations are seasonal and the respondents have to undertake other works in the off seasons. One of the disappointing feature of the financial status of the respondents is that they do not have a regular income, and their occupation is also very much dependent on unpredictable factors like good climate, good monsoon etc.

Table 6.1: Occupation of the Head of the household.

Occupation of the head of the household	*Frequency*	*Per cent*
Agriculture labour	145	19.5
Unskilled labour	412	54.9
Work in factory (skilled labour)	45	6.0
Self-employed (petty shop)	13	1.7
Nothing fixed/keep on changing occupation	31	4.1
Vendor and hawker	85	11.3
Any other	6	0.8
NADK	13	1.7
Total	**750**	**100.0**

Occupational status of the head of the household is an important variable in determining the social and economic status of the family. Uneducated and unskilled people find hardly any space in the organised sector. Business and self-employment are also rare options for the illiterate population. The only option available for such people seems to be agricultural labour and unskilled part-time occupations during the off seasons. These occupations are labour intensive. Most of the unskilled jobs are remunerated as daily wages. They have to work every day and they will have very hard time when they fall sick and cannot go to work.

We see from the Table 6.1 that nearly 75 per cent of the heads of the household are engaged in unskilled or agricultural occupation. Only 6 per cent of the respondents are skilled labourers, while 11.3 per cent of the heads of the family are hawkers or vendors.

Occupationally the entire families of the respondents seem to be agricultural or unskilled daily labourers. Since majority of the landless labourers are illiterate they remain unskilled and are forced to look for unskilled agricultural occupations that yield poor income. The invariable relationship between illiteracy, unemployment and poverty is once again revealed in the Table 6.1. The mental horizon of the illiterate parents remain limited and they don't see much better future for their children, especially the girl children.

Table 6.2 : Income of the family.

Income of the family	*Income in actual (Rs.)*					*Total*
(Rs.)	*0-2000*	*2001-4000*	*4001-6000*	*6001–8000*	*NADK*	
0-2000	131	294	3			428
2001-4000		156	85	1		242
4001-6000			30	21		51
6001-8000				18		18
8001 or above				1		1
NADK					10	10
Total	**131**	**450**	**118**	**41**	**10**	**750**

The calculation of monthly income for the landless agricultural labourers is a difficult one. First of all these labourers do not have a regular income. Most of them are paid on daily basis and they lose the day's wage whenever they remain absent due to illness. However, this query was asked repeatedly and all the efforts were made to ascertain the monthly income of the respondents.

Income of the family is what the respondents have disclosed of their average monthly income inclusive of all the non-agricultural earnings of the family members (from their own land) and income in actual refers to the total monthly income of the family including the agricultural income. Therefore, the actual income looks higher than the income disclosed. Since agricultural income is not steady a little caution is applied in calculating this income.

We see from the Table that nearly 60 per cent of the respondents have their disclosed monthly income as below Rs. 2000 while over 60 per cent of their actual monthly income is between Rs. 2000 to Rs. 4000. Only 10 per cent of the respondents have their family income more than Rs. 4000 per month which means 90 per cent of the respondents have their annual income below Rs. 48,000. Since the average number of members in a family is 5, this income is found insufficient to meet the daily needs of the family.

Table 6.3 : Per capita income of the family.

Per capita Family income	*Family members actual*			
	Less than 3 members	*Between 4 to 6 members*	*7 or above*	*Total*
0-500	4	162	75	241
501-1000	129	206	74	409
1001-1500	56	10	16	82
1501-2000	4			4
2001-2500	2			2
2501-3000	1	1		2
NADK	8	2		10
Total	**204**	**381**	**165**	**750**

Per capita (monthly) income of the respondents is calculated on the basis of their aggregate family income and the number of family members. Some families with higher income are found to have very meagre per capita income due to their large size of the families. To maintain the financial security of the family, it is important to keep the family size small.

Over 30 per cent of the respondents have the per capita income below Rs. 500 and 85 per cent of the respondents have the per capita income less than Rs. 1000. Only 15 per cent of the respondents have per capita income above Rs. 1000. It is also seen that smaller families have higher per capita income. Almost 50 per cent of the families with more than 7 members have the per capita income below Rs. 500. Out of 204 families with less than three members, only four families have the per capita income less than Rs. 500.

Poor families are large families. The average size of the families below poverty line is above five. Illiterate parents are reluctant to adopt any family planning methods. They are also hesitant to educate their daughters. They want their girls to get married at the earliest and boys to enter into some unskilled occupation. Thus illiteracy, large families, unemployment and underemployment and low per capita income complete the vicious circle of poverty.

Table 6.4 : Land owned by the respondents

Income	*Does family own some land*			*Total*
	Yes	*Not sure*	*No*	
0-2000	5	3	135	143
2001-4000	39	2	285	326
4001-6000	4		199	203
6001-8000	4		55	59
8001 or above	2		17	19
Total	**54**	**5**	**691**	**750**

Land is the most valuable asset for the landless labourers. As long as they remain illiterate and unskilled, they are unable to get an alternative occupation and agricultural work is the only option. Therefore, they wish to invest on land which is the only productive means. When the landless labourers are able to save any amount they think of purchasing agricultural land. Once they own land they are no more considered as landless labourers. A few respondents have acquired land by investing their entire savings and by taking loans. Still they are going to work in others' fields. The plot they have acquired is very small and the cultivation in that plot is not sufficient for their daily living. They have a loan to repay, so they have to work hard.

We can see from the Table 6.4 that only 7 per cent of the respondents have own land. Over 90 per cent of the respondents are landless. Those who are acquired land have acquired it recently by taking loans. Those who have land have relatively better family income. We have seen from the previous table that small families have better per capita income and a higher family income. Similarly families with higher income have saved money for investing for land. It is not known whether their family income rose after the purchase of land or they purchased the land after having secured better income status. What is asserted by this finding is the invariable relationship between the ownership of land and better family income.

Table 6.5 : Personal Income of the respondents.

Income of the respondent	*Frequency*	*Per cent*
0-500	122	16.3
501-1000	336	44.8
1001-1500	220	29.3
1501-2000	53	7.1
2001-2500	13	1.7
2501-3000	6	0.8
Total	**750**	**100.0**

It is seen from the Table 6.5 that 16.3 per cent of the respondents earn Rs. 500 or less per month and 44.8 per cent of the respondents earn between Rs. 500 to Rs. 1000 per month. The other respondents (29.3 %) earn between Rs. 1000 to Rs. 1500 per month. Nearly 10 per cent of the respondents earn more than Rs. 1500 as personal income. Over 60 per cent of the respondents earn below Rs. 1000 per month which means below Rs. 40 per day. It is much below the minimum wage. Minimum wage for unskilled agricultural occupations in Delhi, U.P and Haryana is between Rs. 70 to Rs. 110. We can see from the table that only 19 respondents secure minimum wages as per the government norms.

Working Conditions of the respondents

The working conditions of the respondents reveal that the landless women labour have seasonal occupation and have engaged in other works in off seasons. In addition to all these works, they are also responsible for all the household works. Rarely do they have freedom to spend the money they earn. Even when they spend their earnings, they spend them only for the general purposes of the family. What they spend upon themselves is minimal. They usually hand over their earnings to their husbands. Since they do not have any bank accounts they keep their savings in the hands of their husbands. In this context the role of self-help groups is significant.

Table 6.6 : Work on land and period of employment.

How often do you on other's land	*Are you working on the same piece of land for generation*				*Total*
	Yes	*Not sure*	*No*	*NADK*	
6 months or more in a year	56	76	74	26	232
3-6 months	73	10	284		367
30 days a year	48	5	87		140
Any other		2			2
NADK		1	6	2	9
Total	**177**	**94**	**451**	**28**	**750**

The primary characteristic of the landless labourer is that they cultivate in others' land for a duration which is less than six months' a year. They seldom occupy the same piece of land the following year. Most of the landless labourers are leading a nomadic way of living. They migrate from one place to another looking for any type of unskilled job. Construction work is the most popular alternate occupation for the landless labourers during the off seasons. Construction works are usually available during the dry season and agricultural operations are mostly done during the monsoon season.

It is seen from the Table 6.6 that less than 25 per cent of the respondents are working on the same piece of land for several generations. Over 60 per cent of the respondents do not work on the same piece of land for generations. 30 per cent of the respondents occupy others' land for more than 6 months a year while nearly 50 per cent of the respondents occupy others' land for three to six months. Nearly 20 per cent of the respondents occupy others' land for 30 days or less in a year.

This Table shows that majority of the respondents (nearly 70 %) work as landless labourers for less than six months in a year confirming a previous finding that the agricultural labour is only seasonal. This seasonal engagement does not satisfy the respondents and they are compelled to find some off seasonal occupations.

Table 6.7 : Other activities of the LWL.

How often do you occupy on other's land	*Do you do other activities* Yes	Not sure	No	Any other	NADK	*Total*
6 months or more in a year	190	1	28		13	232
3-6 months	228		114		25	367
30 days a year	46		87	5	2	140
Any other			2			2
NADK		2	7			9
Total	**464**	**3**	**238**	**5**	**40**	**750**

Agricultural work is a seasonal occupation by nature. Agricultural income is also seasonal. Since most of the agricultural holdings in the States of Haryana, U.P. and Delhi are comparatively larger in size, they earn enough for the whole year. They do preserve the agricultural produce required for the whole year. They hire the landless labourers during the harvesting as well as the sowing seasons. These labourers are paid on daily basis.

We see from the Table 6.7 that 60 per cent of the respondents do other activities to complement their seasonal agricultural occupation. Out of 464 respondents who are engaged in other activities, 228 respondents are engaged in agricultural occupations for 3 to 6 months, 190 are engaged in agricultural jobs in others' land for over 6 months. It is seen that among the respondents who are engaged in agricultural operation for less than 30 days a year, the majority are not engaged in other occupations.

It shows that these respondents are engaged in the agricultural operations only casually, not out of financial necessity and they do not need to look for supplementary source of income in the off seasons. Engagement in other activities depends upon the need of the family, skill and convenience of the respondents. It is interesting to see that the respondents who are engaged in seasonal agricultural works for six months or more are the same people who are engaged in other activities. From this finding we can infer that the need of the landless women labour is so pressing that they try to get any unskilled engagement to supplement their seasonal income.

Table 6.8 : Kind of other works undertaken by the respondents

What kind of work	*Per capita Family income*							*Total*
	0-500	*501-1000*	*1001-1500*	*1501-2000*	*2001-2500*	*2501-3000*	*NADK*	
Labour as construction worker	88	75	32		2			197
Handicraft activity	5	24						29
Work in factory	3							3
Domestic work	18	18	16	2			8	62
Nothing is fixed	54	111	4					169
Any other	2	3	5					10
NADK	71	178	25	2		2	2	280
Total	**241**	**409**	**82**	**4**	**2**	**2**	**10**	**750**

Table6.8 indicates that over 25 per cent of the respondents are working as construction workers during the off seasons, and majority of them earn less than Rs. 1000 per month from such occupation. Over 20 per cent of the respondents are engaged in any unskilled daily labour available and there are no fixed occupations for them. Their monthly income is mostly between Rs. 500 to Rs. 1000. Nearly 10 per cent of the respondents have found off-seasonal occupation as domestic workers and most of them earn a monthly income more than Rs. 500. Only 5 per cent of the respondents are engaged in other off-seasonal occupations like handicrafts activities, work in the factories etc. Over 35 per cent of the respondents are not engaged in any alternate occupations in the off seasons.

Majority of the respondents are engaged in construction works during the off seasons. Agricultural operations are held mainly during the monsoon seasons and construction works are mainly done during the dry seasons. Monsoon is off-season for construction works. Much of the construction works are undertaken by the building contractors who recruit the easily available landless women labour as daily labours for the unskilled works. They seldom fight for the rights of a worker, such as minimum wage, workman's compensation, maternity leave, gratuity, increment, provident fund, ESI benefit etc. During the monsoon season these workers will go back to their respective villages to undertake the traditionally contracted agricultural works.

Table 6.9 : Involvement in Household Activities.

Sl. No.	*Involvement in Household Activities*	*Frequency*	*(%)*
1.	Cooking, cleaning, washing	732	97.61
2.	Looking after children, elderly and guest	471	62.83
3.	Looking after cattle	435	58.04
4.	Stitching/Knitting	82	10.87
5.	Singing, dancing and sitting with friends	82	10.87
6.	Studying and getting training	2	0.22
7	Supervising children's home work	11	1.52

Apart from the seasonal agricultural works and off-seasonal

supplementary works, the respondents have to discharge a number of household activities. It can be seen from the Table 6.9 that 97.61 per cent of the respondents are doing the daily domestic routine like cooking, cleaning and washing. 62.83 per cent of the respondents have look to after the children, the elderly and the guests. 58.04 per cent of the respondents have to look after the cattle. Only 10.87 per cent of the respondents are engaged in some leisure time activities (hobbies) like stitching, knitting, singing, dancing and sitting with friends. Only 11 respondents spare time to supervise their children's home work. It is seen that only 2 respondents are studying and getting some vocational training in some non-agricultural trade.

Domestic responsibilities are inseparable routine of the rural women, whether they are working or non-working. This is one of the reasons why rural women simply prefer to settle down in life as simple housewives. Housewives are undertaking silently the entire productive as well as non-productive household responsibilities. Nobody has ever questioned these responsibilities of women. In large size families, domestic duties like cleaning, cooking, washing, looking after the children and the elderly, fetching water and fuel, preparing tiffin for husband and children, and supervising the education of children alone consume the entire day time of the women. It is unbelievable to see that after discharging all these responsibilities the landless women labour have found time and convenience to undertake both seasonal agricultural works as well as off seasonal non-agricultural works.

Table 6.10 : What the respondents do with their income.

What do you do with your income	*Frequency*	*%*
Spend in family	380	50.7
Spend on food of self and children	250	33.3
Spend on children's education	3	0.4
Spend on paying bank debts	4	0.5
Spend on additional expenditure	11	1.5
Spend on savings	4	0.5
Nothing is fixed	72	9.6
NADK	26	3.5
Total	**750**	**100.0**

It is generally found that women have little right over the spending of their own earnings. The poor women venture out in the world of work due to great financial constraints of the household. Whatever the little earnings brought by women are spent in the family and for the food.

This Table 6.10 gives us information about how the respondents spend their income. 84 per cent of the respondents spend their income in the family for food expenses. This confirms the general assumption that landless women labour are leading a lifestyle of hand to mouth sustenance. Less than 1 per cent is spent for the education of the children, paying bank the debts, and for savings. Nearly 10 per cent of the respondents do not have any fixed expenditure pattern.

Much of their earnings are spent in their family and for food. The families of landless women labour depend largely on the income of the women. The earnings of the respondents are very important for survival of their families. The work of female members is very important in poor families. In rural areas, women rarely go out of home for any work outside home. Usually rural women are housewives. The poor illiterate women are happy to live like simple housewives. If they go out of home for any work, it is due to sheer necessity of survival. When their husbands are unable to earn enough to maintain the family, the rural women get out rendering a helping hand to their partners. They do these works not forgoing the domestic duties but after completing these works. Thus the burden of working women in rural areas is doubled.

Table 6.11 : What do the husbands do with the income of LWL.

What do your husband do with your income	*Frequency*	*Per cent*
They take it and I do not know what they do with it	48	6.4
Take it and utilize in the family	312	41.6
Take it as everyone contributes	1	0.1
Take some amount and give some to me	8	1.1
They save it	19	2.5
Give it to me for saving	34	4.5
They have no concern with it	258	34.4
NADK	70	9.4
Total	**750**	**100.0**

It is a tradition in rural areas that the men hold property rights and the women have little share in the monetary affairs of the family. Usually the respondents hand over their earnings to their husbands. In the Table 6.11, we learn how the husbands of the respondents spend their earnings. 41.6 per cent of the respondents believe that their husbands take the money and utilise it for meeting various expenses of the family. 34.4 per cent of the respondents have disclosed that their husbands have no concern with their earnings. 7 per cent of the respondents said that their husbands would save the money or entrust the same to themselves for saving. Only 6.4 per cent of the respondents have told that they do not know what their husbands would do with their earnings.

It can be seen that all the respondents are very positive about the attitude of their husbands regarding the spending of their earnings. Combining this finding with the previous one, we can conclude that whether it is spent by the respondents or their husbands the purpose of the expenditure does not change. The lion's share is spent for the family and primarily for food expenses. What is spent on education, savings and other investments is very meagre.

Concluding Remarks

Economic and occupational profile of landless women labour is described in this chapter. Most of the heads of the household are engaged in unskilled or agricultural occupation. Occupationally the entire families of the respondents are agricultural or unskilled daily labourers. Most of the respondents have their monthly income below Rs. 2000. Most of the respondents have their annual income below Rs. 48,000. Majority of the respondents have the per capita income less than Rs. 1000 which means below Rs. 40 per day much below minimum wages. Poor families are large families. The average size of the families below poverty line is above five. Majority of the respondents are landless.

Majority of the landless women labour do work for less than six months a year. Majority of the respondents do other activities to complement their seasonal agricultural occupation. Majority of the respondents are engaged in construction works during the off-seasons. Apart from the seasonal agricultural works and off-seasonal supplementary works, most of the respondents have to discharge a number of household activities like cooking, cleaning and washing, looking after the children, the elderly and the guests and looking after the cattle. Domestic responsibilities are inseparable routine of the rural women, whether they are working or non-working. This is one of the reasons why rural women simply prefer to settle down in life as simple housewives.

Majority of the respondents spend their income in the family for food expenses. The families of landless women labour depend largely on the income of the women. The earnings of the respondents are very important for survival of their families. The work of female members is very important in poor families. All the respondents are very positive about the attitude of their husbands regarding the spending of their earnings. The lion's share is spent for the family and primarily for food expenses. What is spent on education, savings and other investments is very meagre.

Chapter 7

PROBLEMS OF LANDLESS WOMEN LABOUR

The problems faced by landless women labour are multifarious. The most crucial problems faced by landless women labour (LWL) are the harassment, wage differential and indebtedness. The disappointing aspect of the situation is that in most of the cases the victims of the social injustice are unable to react or get the assistance of legal machinery to reinstate justice. The situation is just accepted as normal both by the oppressors as well as the victims. Since no complaints are registered, the police are unable to intervene. For the victims, their fear of loss of livelihood prevents them from complaining against the landlords. Since these poor labourers are unskilled and therefore unable to look for any alternative occupation, they bear the harassment as part of their normal working condition. The anchor of indebtedness halts the landless women labour from taking bold decisions like changing the employer or migrating to far away places.

Harassment at Workplace

The most common workplace harassment is sexual harassment. Majority of the landless women labour belong to the scheduled caste and the scheduled tribe. Tradition and the customs of the ancient Hindu order permit the sexual rights of the higher caste men over the lower caste women. Even if strict legislative measures are passed in India, the landlords in the remote villages tend to exploit the ignorance and illiteracy of the women labourer and make them believe that securing the favour and blessing of the landlords by any means is necessary for remaining in the job. Reporting rate is much less compared to the occurrence rate of the incidence of sexual harassment.

Table 7.1: Harassment at workplace.

Age of the respondent (years)	*Is workplace harassment common among Landless Women Labour*				*Total*
	Yes	*Not sure*	*No*	*NADK*	
20-25	76	126	6	39	247
26-30	22	55	4	37	118
31-35	61	28		49	138
36-40	17	22		6	45
41-45	39	18		11	68
46-50	14	11		1	26
51 or more	32	61	2	13	108
Total	**261**	**321**	**12**	**156**	**750**

Workplace harassment is very common among the illiterate workforce especially landless and the domestic labours. They are usually kept under threat of various types. The employers use the threat of suspension or dismissal from the job. The co-workers use physical threat to harass the women labours. Thus the victims are intimidated to remain silent about the harassment. It was found from different discussions with the respondents that they were reluctant to answer any direct question on work place harassment. Therefore, different indirect queries were included in the questionnaire to explore into the real situation of workplace harassment. The first attempt in this regard was just asking a general question whether workplace harassment is common among the landless women labour. This question has generalised the individual experiences of the respondents and they felt more comfortable to say yes or no to this statement.

We see from the Table 7.1 that only 12 respondents could emphatically say 'no' with regard to the incidence of workplace harassment. 156 respondents who did not respond to the query are non-working at the time of the research. Over 35 per cent of the respondents have reported the incidence of workplace harassment and over 40 per cent of the respondents are not sure about the happenings of harassment or have not recognised certain behaviour as harassment. The observation and probing of the research investigators have confirmed the occurrence of workplace harassment in majority of the cases.

Table 7.2 : Nature of harassment.

Any harassment in fields	*Frequency*	*(%)*
A matter of routine	27	3.6
People take advantage all the times	106	14.1
Men are always like that but I am careful	41	5.5
Feel insecure	145	19.3
Very good work atmosphere	55	7.3
Any other	7	0.9
NADK	369	49.3
Total	**750**	**100.0**

Another indirect enquiry was, asking about the nature of harassment the women usually face at workplace. This question has made the respondents comfortable enough to disclose the nature of their harassing experiences without personally relating them. The respondents were ready to speak about others' experiences as if it reflects the general situation of women at the workplace. Even if the narrations are not their own personal experiences, it is very much possible that some of the incidences are real projections of own experiences. It is also shown that women are willing to disclose threatening experiences provided that an encouraging environment is created.

Over 40 per cent of the respondents have revealed the nature of harassment faced by them. 19.3 per cent of the respondents have disclosed that they feel insecure at the workplace due to harassment. 14.1 per cent of the respondents feel that the people are taking advantages all the time. Only 7.3 per cent of the respondents have reported good work atmosphere. All the incidents reported were the events of sexual harassment. 49.2 per cent of the respondents have not reported any incidents of workplace harassment. While we analyse the next Table 7.3 we can find that the non-reporting does not mean non-occurrence.

Table 7.3 : Age of the respondents and the workplace harassment.

Any harassment in fields	*Age of the respondent (years)*							
	20-25	*26-30*	*31-35*	*36-40*	*41-45*	*46-50*	*51 or more*	*Total*
A matter of routine	13	5		3	2	2	2	27
People take advantage all the times	18	4	12	7	20	7	38	106
Men are always like that but I am careful	2		32	3	4			41
Feel insecure	46	31	28	7	7	13	13	145
Very good work atmosphere	30	15	2	2	6			55
Any other		3		3			1	7
NADK	138	60	64	20	29	4	54	369
Total	**247**	**118**	**138**	**45**	**68**	**26**	**108**	**750**

An attempt is made to relate the age of the respondents and workplace harassment. No significant relationship is established between age and harassment. All the respondents regardless the age differences have experienced harassment. However, it can be seen from the Table 7.3 that more of the respondents who are younger in age face harassment as a matter of routine and also feel insecure at the workplace. It is also seen that younger respondents feel good work environment compared to others.

The relationship between age of the respondents and reaction to workplace harassment is shown in the Table 7.4. It is seen from the table that younger respondents are more reactive to harassment than the elder ones. It may be inferred that younger respondents face more harassment. Another inference is that older respondents have got used to the situation and prefer not to react.

Table 7.4 : Age of the respondents and reaction to harassment.

Reaction to harassment	*Age of the respondent (years)*							*Total*
	20-25	*26-30*	*31-35*	*36-40*	*41-45*	*46-50*	*51 or more*	
Went to Sarpancha or police	2	10		1	4			17
Complain to elders in area	15	7	64	8	5		8	107
Talk to friends and family	25	2	5		18	1	6	57
Curse the guilty	13	2	2		9			26
Remained silent	87	45	53	19	10	19	45	278
NADK	105	52	14	17	22	6	49	265
Total	**247**	**118**	**138**	**45**	**68**	**26**	**108**	**750**

Table 7.5 : Reaction to harassment.

Reaction to harassment	*Frequency·*	*(%)*
Went to Sarpancha or police	17	2.3
Complain to elders in area	107	14.3
Talk to friends and family	57	7.6
Curse the guilty	26	3.5
Remained silent	278	37.1
NADK	265	35.2
Total	**750**	**100.0**

Since most of the questions regarding workplace harassment were indirect ones, some inconsistencies are visible when we compare the responses to the same question asked in different ways. Neither compulsion nor corrections are made to the responses rendered by the respondents regarding workplace harassment. The most direct questions about the harassment have elicited little positive response. What is rational in such situation is to comprehend the totality of the situation by putting together the information received to various enquiries about the harassment. From Table 7.5 we can assert that nearly 65 per cent of the respondents have faced workplace harassment and 37.6 per cent of the respondents preferred to remain silent about it. Only 2.3 per cent of the respondents were ready to complain against the assailant to the Sarpancha or the Police. 21.9 per cent of the respondents disclosed the incidence to some elders or friends while 3.5 per cent of the respondents cursed the guilty and refused to disclose to anybody. The finding of this Table 7.5 supplements to the findings of the previous two tables by filling some vacuum. This explains situation why the reporting of the workplace harassment is rare.

For reasons unknown majority of the victims of social injustice remain silent. Either they are afraid of losing the job, or lost faith in the legal machinery, or don't wish to become notorious, or got used to and became insensitive to injustice. The primary objective of this study is to sensitise both the governmental and non-governmental agencies as well as the general public about the pathetic situation of the victims of social injustice, the landless women labour.

Table 7.6 : What Government should do prevent harassment?

Sl.No.	*What Government should do prevent harassment?*	*Frequency*	*(%)*
1.	Appoint officers	52	6.96
2.	Punish the offenders	41	5.43
	Total	**93**	**12.39**

Very few respondents answered to this query. 12.39 per cent of the respondents are of the opinion that the Government should appoint some inspectors to check the incidence of workplace harassment or take some steps to punish the offenders to prevent the occurrence of workplace harassment. In vast majority of cases, the respondents are not aware of any role played by Government in these situations. They blame themselves for not being careful enough to be victimised or remain silent. Lack of basic education and proper awareness regarding the existing legal machinery contribute to this situation. Government should take up some creative step in accordance with the recent Supreme Court guidelines regarding sexual harassment at workplace extending its scope to the unorganised agricultural sector.

Wage differential of LWL

Another serious problem faced by landless women labour is the prevailing wage differential. Unlike the industrial sector which is largely organised, wage difference is very much prevalent in the unorganised agricultural sector. Women, all over India, receive fewer wages for the same kind of work done by men in the same field. Sometimes women are assigned with more labour intensive tasks while their male counter part undertakes more technical (less labour intensive) operations. Often the skilled operations are less labour intensive compared to the unskilled ones. Illiteracy of the respondents contributes to the injustice done against them. They seldom react against this injustice for fear of losing job.

Table 7.7 : Lower wages of LWL.

Is your income lesser than male counterpart	*Frequency*	*(%)*
Yes	195	26.0
Not sure	282	37.6
No	119	15.9
NADK	154	20.5
Total	**750**	**100.0**

Paying lower wages to women labourers in the agricultural sector is a common practice in India. Minimum Wages Act ensures equal pay for men and women for the same kind of work. Equality in payment is also a constitutional right. However, the illiterate women remain helpless and get enforced this fundamental right. In the organised sector and in the urban areas equality of payment of wages is being recognised. It is partly because of the applicability of the labour law provisions in the organised sector and partly because of the better educational status of women labourers in urban areas. We see from the Table 7.7 that 26 per cent of the respondents are clearly aware of the fact that they receive lower wages compared to their male counterpart. This awareness is a key factor for creative action. While we analyse the reaction we can see that very few dared to react. 37.6 per cent are not sure whether there is any difference in the wages between men and women. Many of the respondents in this category have their own justification for a higher wages for their male counter part. 20.5 per cent of the respondents were not working at the time of the survey, hence did not respond to this query. Only 15.9 per cent of the respondents receive equal wages for their work in comparison to their male counterpart.

Table 7.8 : Marital status of the respondents and wage differential.

Marital status	*Is your income lesser than male counterpart*				*Total*
	Yes	*Not sure*	*No*	*NADK*	
Single	6	10	19	9	44
Married	185	228	85	122	620
Widow	4	44	15	23	86
Total	**195**	**282**	**119**	**154**	**750**

It can be seen from the Table 7.8 that difference in the wages is more among the married respondents compared to the corresponding proportion among the unmarried respondents and the widows. Since both the husbands and wives work in the same fields, the custom of discriminatory payment is rather accepted by the wives. Another inference is that married respondents are more aware of the wage differential compared to the unmarried ones.

Table 7.9 : Income of the respondents and wage differential.

Education of the respondent	*Is your income lesser than male counterpart*				*Total*
	Yes	*Not sure*	*No*	*NADK*	
Illiterate	189	226	93	125	633
Upto primary	6	54	26	28	114
NADK		2		1	3
Total	**195**	**282**	**119**	**154**	**750**

A clear relationship is established between the educational status of the respondents and the experience of wage differential. The illiterate respondents experience more wage differential compared to the literate respondents. It is easy to discriminate the illiterate women in comparison to the literate ones. This indicates to an effective strategy to fight against wage differential that is to educate the illiterate women labours and make them literate. Literacy is the power that could empower the weak to fight against injustice.

Table 7.10 : Wage differential.

How much is different?	*Frequency*	*(%)*
It is half	15	2.0
It is 3/4th	27	3.6
It is 10% less	106	14.1
It is little less	18	2.4
It is less but cannot calculate	37	4.9
Any other	2	.3
NADK	545	72.7
Total	**750**	**100.0**

This Table 7.10 fills some gap found in the previous table. From this table we can clearly see that 37.3 per cent of the respondents are aware of the fact that their wages are lower than that of the male counterpart. 14.1 per cent of the respondents have reported that their wages are 10 per cent less than that of their male counterpart. 5.6 per cent of the respondents have disclosed that their wages are ¾ or lesser compared to that of the male labourers. Nearly 8 per cent of the respondents are sure that their wages are lower but are not able to calculate it.

Landless women labours are generally timid to ask the employer about the wage differential. Even if they ask they are not heard. We see from the Table 7.11 that only 6.4 per cent of the respondents were bold enough to ask the employer why there is difference in the wages between men and women. Over 36.3 per cent of the respondents either never thought of asking or were not dare enough

Table 7.11 : Did you ask the employer about this wage differential between male and female landless labourers

Have you asked employer why is it less?	*Frequency*	*(%)*
Yes	48	6.4
Asked indirectly	4	0.5
Could not dare to ask	108	14.4
It never came to mind	164	21.9
NADK	426	56.8
Total	**750**	**100.0**

to ask. What is revealed indirectly in this table is that above 40 per cent of the respondents receive lower wages compared to their male counterpart. Majority of the respondents who experience wage differential do not ask for equal wages or don't bother about asking due to many reasons. They are either afraid of dismissal or recognise for themselves the superiority of male labourer in all the situations both inside as well as outside home or are happy with what they get at present. The primary observation in this regard is that in most of the cases the respondents are not aware of their right for equal wages for equal work. All other reasons are secondary. Often women prefer peaceful negotiations at the workplace avoiding every chance of friction with male co-workers as well as male supervisors. In many cases both husbands are wives are employed in the same field and wives are happy to know that their husbands are earning better than themselves and hence complaining against wage differential never comes in their mind.

Only 10 per cent of the respondents received some answers for their query regarding the wage differential between male and female landless labourers. Among all the unreasonable responses mentioned in the Table 7.12 the reference to the poor or lesser quality of women's work was the most frequent one, followed by the inferior quality of the overall performance of women and the inferior quality of women's work. The inability of women to undertake certain operations was the rarest response. The finding of this Table 7.12 supports the investigator's view regarding the

Table 7.12 : Reason given by employer.

Reasons given by the employer	*Frequency*	*(%)*
Women's work is quality-wise inferior	15	2.0
Women's work is quality-wise lesser	34	4.5
Women's overall performance is inferior	19	2.5
Women cannot do everything that men can do	1	0.1
Women are inferior in everyway	2	0.3
Neither reason was asked nor given	5	0.7
Any other	2	0.3
NADK	672	89.6
Total	**750**	**100.0**

ignorance and illiteracy of landless women labour who could be silenced by such irrational answers. Since 85 per cent of the respondents were illiterate, the employers could easily satisfy them with irrational answers. The reasons given by the employers confirm the prevailing stereotypes regarding the women's work. Landless women labours seem to be satisfied with these explanations. These explanations have simply reinforced the false self-image of the respondents who silently bore the injustice done against them. Illiterate and ignorant women are thus victimised. Unless organised efforts are undertaken to impart literacy and basic education victims of social injustice cannot be helped in any way.

Table 7.13 : What steps are taken by LWL against lesser wages.

Have you asked employer why is it less?	*What did you take ?*			
	Discussed with family members	*Any other*	*NADK*	*Total*
Yes			48	48
Asked indirectly			4	4
Could not dare to ask	24		84	108
It never came to mind			164	164
NADK		1	425	426
Total	**24**	**1**	**725**	**750**

Table 7.13 shows that 24 respondents discussed the matter with the family members. All these respondents could not dare to ask the employer. 48 respondents dared to ask the employer why they were paid less. Most of the respondents remained inactive with regard to less wages paid to them. Those who asked were sent back with unreasonable answers. None could take up any effective step with regard to fewer wage paid to them.

Indebtedness

Rural indebtedness is the most common problem of the landless labourers. Since these people are illiterate, they remain ignorant about various government schemes for the poor. They are not aware about various credit schemes of NABARD for the women below poverty line. Credit formation through self-help groups is successful among the literate women. NGOs are mostly working with the women who are settled. Government schemes and bank loans are also available for the agricultural families who have proper documents. Landless labours do not have land and often lack documents to show permanent residential proof. The primary source of credit known to the landless women labour is the money-lenders. The credit sought by the landless labourers is mainly for unproductive purposes and the security given by these people often get lost due to non-payment of the loan taken. The following tables describe the status of loan taken by the respondents.

Table 7.14 : Indebtedness.

Income of the family	*Have you ever taken loan*				*Total*
	Yes	*Not sure*	*No*	*NADK*	
0-2000	84	16	324	4	428
2001-4000	62	2	173	5	242
4001-6000	20		31		51
6001-8000			18		18
8001 or above			1		1
NADK			10		10
Total	**166**	**18**	**557**	**9**	**750**

We see from the Table 7.14 that 166 respondents have taken loan and another 18 women have taken some borrowings which they are not sure whether they are debt in real sense or not. It is expected that those families with lower income have incurred debt and their ability to repay the same is very much limited.

Table 7.15 : Purpose of Loan.

Sl.No.	*Purpose of loan*	*Frequency*	*(%)*
1.	Marriage	73	9.78
2.	Purchase of land	78	10.43
3.	House construction	7	0.87
4.	Purchase of cattle	7	0.87
5.	Medical care	3	0.43
6.	To pay debts	2	0.22
7.	Any other	8	1.09
	Total	**178**	**23.70**

Landless labours take loans for expenses related with marriage, purchase of land, house construction, purchase of cattle, medicine purchase and to repay old debts. Even if they take loans often, they do not disclose them. They are reluctant to approach the bank or government agencics for loans. Due to a number of formalities, the illiterate women are often unable to avail the benefits of various welfare schemes. Since their credibility to repay the loans is not convincing the bankers hesitate to lend loans to them. Therefore, they are compelled to take loans from the money lenders with a high percentage of interest. The money lenders on the other hand take away all the amounts the landless labours able to save.

We see from the Table 7.15 that only 23.7 per cent of the respondents have taken loan and 10.43 per cent of the respondents have taken loan to purchase land which is a progressive trend. Another 9.78 per cent of the respondents have taken loan for meeting the expenses of marriage. Less than 4 per cent of the respondents have incurred debt for other purposes like house construction, purchase of cattle, medical care, and to pay back old debts. We can find a better picture of the status of the loan taken by the respondents from the next Table 7.16.

Table 7.16 : Status of Loan.

Sl.No.	Purpose of loan	Marriage	Purchase of land	House construction	Purchase of cattle	Medical care	To pay debts	Any other	Total	(%)
A	**Source of loan**									
1.	Bank	13	7	2	3	0	0	2	25	3.48
2.	Employer	39	0	0	0	0	0	0	39	5.22
3.	Money-lender	21	70	5	3	3	2	2	106	14.13
4.	Relative/friends	0	0	0	0	0	0	5	5	0.65
5.	Friend	0	2	0	0	0	0	0	2	0.22
6.	NADK	677	672	743	743	747	748	742	572	76.30
B	**Amount of loan (Rs.)**									
1.	0-5,000	0	10	3	2	2	2	7	24	3.26
2.	5,001-10,000	5	28	2	2	0	0	0	36	4.78
3.	10,001-15,000	49	2	0	0	0	0	0	51	6.74
4.	15,001-20,000	5	38	0	0	0	0	0	42	5.65
5.	20,001-25,000	0	0	2	0	0	0	2	3	0.43
6.	25,001-30,000	0	2	0	2	0	0	0	3	0.43
7.	30,001-35,000	15	0	0	2	2	0	0	18	2.39
8.	NADK	577	672	743	743	747	748	742	572	76.30
C	**Period of loan**									
1.	Less than 1 year	36	18	5	0	0	2	7	67	8.91
2.	1 – 3 years	34	60	2	2	3	0	2	103	13.70
3.	NADK	680	672	743	748	747	748	742	580	77.39

(Contd...)

(Contd...)

D	**Rate of Interest**	0	0	0	0	0	0	0	0	–
1.	0-4 per cent monthly	36	0	7	2	0	0	2	46	6.09
2.	4-8 per cent monthly	34	54	0	3	0	2	2	95	12.61
3.	12 per cent or more	0	0	0	0	2	0	0	2	0.22
4.	NADK	680	696	743	745	748	748	747	608	81.09
E	**Status of loan**									
1.	Returned	15	18	2	3	2	0	2	41	5.43
2.	Returning	18	39	2	0	2	2	0	62	8.26
3.	Not returned	36	15	3	3	0	0	2	59	7.83
4.	NADK	682	678	743	743	747	748	747	589	78.48
	Total	**750**	**750**	**750**	**750**	**750**	**750**	**750**	**750**	**100**

This Table 7.16 describes the sources of loan, amount of loan taken, period of loan, rate of interest and the present status of loan taken by the landless women labour purpose wise. We learn from this table that the respondents have taken loan for meeting the expenses of the marriage mostly from their employer, between Rs. 10,000 to 15,000 for a period less than one year and for less than 4 per cent interest per month. It is also seen that most of these loans are not returned. The respondents have taken loan for purchase of land mostly from the money-lenders, between Rs. 15,000 to 20,000 for a period more than one year and for 4–8 per cent interest per month. It is seen that most of these loans are being returned.

It is also seen that the most popular source of loan is money-lenders, the respondents take an average of Rs. 10,000 to 20,000 as loans, for a period of one to three years, at the rate of 4 to 8 per cent per month and majority of them are returning or have returned the loan.

Concluding Remarks

The problems faced by landless women labour are multifarious. The most crucial problems faced by LWL are the harassment, wage differential and indebtedness. Most of the respondents have faced workplace harassment. All the incidents reported were the events of sexual harassment. Majority of the victims of social injustice remain silent. Majority of the respondents who experience wage differential do not ask for equal wages or don't bother about asking. Most of the respondents are not aware of their right for equal wages for equal work. Often women prefer peaceful negotiations at the workplace avoiding every chance of friction with male co-workers as well as male supervisors. Only a few of the respondents received some answers for their query regarding the wage differential between male and female landless labourers. Among all the unreasonable responses the reference to the poor or lesser quality of women's work was the most frequent one, followed by the inferior quality of the overall performance of women and the inferior quality of women's work. The reasons given by the employers confirm the prevailing stereotypes regarding the women's work.

Rural indebtedness is the most common problem of the landless labourers. The respondents have taken loan for meeting the expenses of the marriage mostly from their employer, between Rs. 10,000 to 15,000 for a period less than one year and for less than 4 per cent interest per month. It is also seen that most of these loans are not returned. The respondents have taken loan for purchase of land mostly from the money-lenders, between Rs. 15,000 to 20,000 for a period more than one year and for 4–8 per cent interest per month. It is seen that most of these loans are being returned.

Chapter 8

ROLE OF GOVERNMENTAL AND NON-GOVERNMENTAL AGENCIES

Panchayati Raj institutions have significant role in the lives of landless labours. Agricultural and rural development programmes are recently been channelled through Panchayat. Extension workers are posted at the block level and are visiting each village on regular intervals. These extension workers bring the development messages to farmers. The landless labourers often miss them. In this chapter we analyse the participation of respondents in the welfare schemes of various governmental and non-governmental agencies. The illiterate landless women labour are found to be ignorant about various government efforts to emancipate them. Therefore, the participation of these people is also very meagre. In the following tables we attempt to analyse the benefits of reservation for women, utilisation of various welfare schemes, and benefit of such schemes for the landless women labour, the opinion of the respondents regarding the government schemes, and the efforts of non-governmental agencies in the uplift of the respondents.

Table 8.1: Benefits of reservation for women.

Is reservation good for women?	*Frequency*	*(%)*
Yes	526	70.2
Not sure	135	18.0
No	37	4.9
NADK	52	6.9
Total	**750**	**100.0**

The Table 8.1 reveals that 70 per cent of the respondents are of the opinion that reservation for women in various fields is very useful. Reservation in legislative bodies, job scenario, educational and vocational institutions would bring out a desirable development in the status of women. Reservation is an effective strategy to ensure the participation of women in political, economic and social fields. Due to the practice of age old patriarchal values, women are systematically kept away from the decision-making bodies at political and economic fields. Managerial level positions in the industrial and service sectors are often not accessible to women. Only a carefully formulated reservation policy would ensure a decent participation of women in every walk of life. This is the insight reflected in the opinion expressed in the Table 8.1.

Table 8.2 : Benefit of welfare schemes.

Do welfare schemes improve women's lives?	*Frequency*	*(%)*
Yes	44	5.9
Not sure	285	38.0
No	302	40.2
NADK	119	15.9
Total	**750**	**100.0**

We can see from the Table 8.2 that 5.9 per cent of the respondents are of the opinion that the welfare schemes of government can improve the lives of women. Majority of the respondents are suspicious about the benefit of welfare schemes in their lives. What is required at this moment is to find ways and means to secure the faith of women in the utility of welfare schemes of government. If the respondents approach the welfare schemes with negative attitudes and prejudice they will not be able to get any benefit out of the schemes.

Over the years the government agencies have been seen as the friends of the employers who are better educated and influential. It is quite natural that the educated citizens have greater access to the welfare schemes and various other services offered by the governmental agencies. The illiterate people tend to believe that the government departments are set up for serving the well off citizens who use various laws and other service delivery systems to suppress the marginalised. Public servants are in an urgent need to get sensitised towards the needs of the landless women labour who are illiterate and vulnerable. Once the governmental agencies have provéd themselves trustworthy, the poor people will boldly approach them for assistance. Unless and until such an attitudinal change is induced among the respondents, no government schemes seem to bring out desirable impact in the lives of landless women labour.

Table 8.3 : Utilisation of existing welfare schemes.

Sl.No.	*Utilisation of existing welfare schemes*	*Heard about it*	*(%)*
1.	EAS (Employment Assurance Scheme)	7	0.87
2.	SJGSY (Swarna Jayanti Gram Swarojgar Yojana)	5	0.65
3.	JGSY (Jawahar Gram Samridhi Yojana)	8	1.09
4.	MWS (Million Wells Scheme)	2	0.22
5.	RLEGP (Rural Labour Employment Guarantee Programme)	7	0.87
6.	TRYSEM (Training for Rural Youth in Self-Employment)	5	0.65
7.	REGS (Rural Employment Guarantee Scheme)	2	0.22
8.	BSY (Balika Samridhi Yojana)	21	2.83
9.	WCP (Women's Component Plan)	5	0.65
10.	Mahila Samakhya	0	0
	Total	**62**	**8.05**

We see from the Table 8.3 that only 8.05 per cent of the respondents have heard about various government schemes for rural development. A vast majority of the respondents are not aware of any government schemes for rural development and practically none of them have ever benefited from such schemes. Among the few schemes, known to the respondents, Balika Samridhi Yojana and Jawahar Gram Samridhi Yojana are more popular than other schemes.

Governmental agencies must give a serious thought about this finding. What the investigator feels is that the procedure of implementation of government schemes should be friendlier to the illiterate mass. The illiterate women are often scared of approaching any governmental agencies for any help. Mass education strategies especially the literacy programme is a pre-condition for the success of any scheme designed for the welfare of the landless women labour. Often the schemes are not addressed to the target groups in the form of strategies meeting their felt needs. The primary need of the landless women labour as reflected in this study is the need for land ownership. We have seen in the Chapter 7 that the respondents have taken more loans for the sake of purchasing land.

Table 8.4 : What Government should do?

Sl.No.	*What Government should do?*	*Frequency*	*(%)*
1.	Allot some land at low prices	571	76.09
2.	Opportunities for employment	385	51.30
3.	Opportunities for education and training	196	26.09
4.	Community health services	46	6.09
5.	House sites	13	1.74
6.	Electricity	28	3.70
7.	Pension for widows	5	0.65
8.	Welfare services	13	1.74

This Table 8.4 shows what the respondents expect the government to do for their sake. Over 75 per cent of the respondents want the government to allot some land for cultivation at a subsidised price. Over 50 per cent of the respondents wish that the government might open up more employment opportunities in the government departments or reserve more jobs for the landless women labour. Some respondents (26 %) were of the opinion that government should create greater opportunities for education and training of landless women labour.

Other expectations of the respondents from the government include provision of community health services, allotment of house sites, electricity, widow pensions etc. Preference is given to the acquisition of land. This discloses the value placed by the respondents in agriculture and cultivable land. For the landless women labour, land is still considered as the most useful and valuable productive resource and want the government to create provision for acquisition of land. This shows that the respondents regard agricultural works as the essential means for livelihood. Keeping this as the first preference the respondents have asked for alternative employment opportunities in service sector or industrial sector.

Even if the respondents are mostly illiterate, they look for alternate occupations, often as a substitute or an alternate for their first preference of land. This finding shows again the general belief that the illiterate mass considers land as the most valuable resource and their regard for physical exertion or labour intensive agricultural operations as the primary means for living.

Table 8.5 : Benefit of NGOs in improving the lives of LWL.

Any NGO working for	*Do NGOs help in improving lives*			*Total*
LWL	*Not sure*	*No*	*NADK*	
Yes		3	3	
Not sure	1	3	2	6
No	55	286	323	664
Any other			4	4
NADK		67	6	73
Total	**56**	**356**	**338**	**750**

This Table 8.5 gives us information about the awareness of the respondents about non-governmental agencies working for the welfare of landless women labour. It is seen that only 3 respondents seem to have heard about any NGOs working for them. No respondents seem to believe in the role of NGOs in improving their lives. This finding points to the fact that very few NGOs are working for the welfare of the landless women labour.

The respondents belong to the marginalised section of the society who are not taken care of both by governmental and the non-governmental agencies. Several reasons can be assigned to this situation. Since the landless women labour are engaged almost all the days in a week in work they are scarcely available to the access of any NGOs. Since these people are overburdened with both the household and the outside occupations, they seldom find time and convenience to attend any meeting held by NGOs. Another reason could be that most of the respondents are illiterate and they do not notice any letters or notice served to them by NGOs. The finding of this table is a reminder for NGOs in the field of rural development regarding the effectiveness of their programmes and activities. They should find out innovative strategies to approach this marginalised section of the society. Carefully planned programmes are to be formulated to uplift landless women labour. These women expect both governmental and non-governmental agencies to work for asserting their rights for cultivable land.

Concluding Remarks

The illiterate landless women labours are found to be ignorant about various government efforts to emancipate them. Therefore, the participation of these people is also very meagre. Most of the respondents are of the opinion that reservation for women in various fields is very useful. Majority of the respondents are suspicious about the benefit of welfare schemes in their lives. Only a few respondents have heard about various government schemes for rural development. A vast majority of the respondents are not aware of any government schemes for rural development and practically none of them have ever benefited from such schemes. Among the few schemes, known to the respondents, Balika Samridhi Yojana and Jawahar Gram Samridhi Yojana are more popular than other schemes.

The primary need of the landless women labour as reflected in this study is the need for land ownership. Majority of the respondents want the government to allot some land for cultivation at a subsidised price. Other expectations of the respondents from the government include opportunities for employment in the government, opening more departments or reserve more jobs, create opportunities for education and training of landless women labour, provision of community health services, allotment of house sites, electricity, widow pensions etc. Preference is given to the acquisition of land. This discloses the value placed by the respondents in agriculture and cultivable land. Hardly anyone has heard about any NGOs working for them. No respondents seem to believe in the role of NGOs in improving their lives. The landless women labour expect both governmental and non-governmental agencies to work for asserting their rights for cultivable land.

Chapter 9
EPILOGUE

Summary of Findings

The findings of the study are summarised in this section. Demographic and social profile of the landless women labourers, economic and occupational profile, problems of landless women labour and the role of governmental and non-governmental agencies are described in this section.

Demographic and Social Profile of Landless Women Labour

Social profile of the respondents includes age, marital status, place of origin, place of destination, caste, head of household, age of the husband, age of the head of the household, sex of the head of the household, education level of the respondent, education level of the husband, education level of the head of the household, education level of the most educated member in the family, desire of the respondents to study, type of family, size of family, opinion of the respondents about marriage, future plans for sons and daughters, interest in village level politics and level of interest in village level politics. It is seen that the social and educational status of landless women labour (LWL) is rather better in Delhi compared to the neighbouring states of U.P. and Haryana.

At least 33 per cent of the respondents are below 25 years of age. 48 per cent of the respondents are below 30 years of age. It can be inferred that agricultural works are labour intensive works and young and healthy persons will only succeed in these unskilled tasks. Older persons can't undertake such works for long hours. 83 per cent of the respondents are married and 6 per cent of the respondents are unmarried. Most of the respondents get married at their twenties and many of them become widows in their fifties. We see none remain unmarried after the age of 25. Early marriage of women is one thing very much encouraged in the rural areas. In Delhi, which is more urbanised than U.P. and Haryana, the age of marriage for women is higher. Therefore, we find more single women in Delhi. Widows are 11 per cent. Among the 108 landless women labour who are above the age of 50, 67 are widows. It confirms the general finding that women survive their spouses and there are more widows than widowers. Since men prefer to marry younger women there is naturally a greater chance for women to survive their men. There are more women without spouses than those with spouses in the age group of 50 and above.

Majority of the respondents are from the State of U.P. From the State of Haryana there are no landless women labour. Out of the 247 respondents who belong to Haryana, 206 come from the State of U.P. Similarly out of 250 respondents from the State of Delhi, 214 are migrants from U.P., Haryana being the richest State in terms of agricultural production, has attracted landless women labour from the State of U.P. Landlessness is a rare phenomenon in the State of Haryana. It is very common in the State of U.P. Majority of the respondents are Hindu by religion. Hindus, especially those who belong to the scheduled and the backward caste are bound to agriculture and allied occupation while the other religious groups in India are more engaged in non-agricultural occupations.

Only 6 respondents belong to the general caste and more than *90 per cent of the landless women labours belong to the backward or scheduled caste and the scheduled tribes.* What is emphasised by this finding is that agricultural operations which are the basic and primary economic activities, the least skilled, the least remunerative were assigned to the backward and the scheduled caste population. Land-holding was traditionally the right of the higher castes and the labourers were of the lower castes. It is well established fact that the scheduled caste and the scheduled tribes except the people of North Eastern States are the least educated, least skilled and the least qualified workforce.

Most of the respondents have their husbands more aged than themselves. Only two women are married to men of younger age. 122 respondents are either unmarried or are widows. The age difference between the couples is on an average of 5 to 10 years. This age difference at the time of marriage was very much accepted in traditional rural communities. 90 per cent of the households are headed by men. Out of the 80 households headed by women, 76 are widows. This finding confirms the fact that Indian society is patriarchal and Indian women accept unconditionally the authority of their husbands or fathers at home. Women head the household only in such a situation where they find no male members at home to be pointed out as the head of the household.

About 85 per cent of the respondents are illiterate. Literacy rate of the landless women labour is nowhere near to the national average. This explains the susceptibility of this vulnerable section of population to easy exploitation. This confirms the general belief that the victims of social justice are the least educated, the marginalised and the most backward section of the society. Only 15 per cent of the respondents have reached up to their primary level of education. The respondents who are literate are of younger age. It sets the progressive trend. *The younger generation is better educated.* Agricultural work is mainly an unskilled job and educational qualification is not a relevant factor for entering into this occupation. Women with higher education do not prefer to remain as daily labour. 50 per cent of the respondents have their husbands who are also illiterate. 35 per cent of the respondents who are illiterate have their husbands literate. The educational status of landless men is definitely higher than that of women. *Literacy level of the husbands is 50 per cent while the literacy level of wives is only 15 per cent.* Parents prefer to educate the boy children and send the girls for work in the field. The illiterate women seldom resist injustice done against them. They are afraid to react against harassment. They tend to respect the customs and traditions and anything in the name of religion, faith and superstitious beliefs would appeal them and bring their obedience.

Mostly the families have literate family members. 274 respondents do not have any other family members who are more educated than themselves. These respondents are illiterate. Educational status of the respondents is higher in the families with better educated members. The parents who are illiterate do not realise the need for educating their children; hence the respondents whose parents are illiterate tend to remain illiterate as in the case of 166 respondents.

Only 11.6 per cent of the respondents have expressed their desire to study. 50 per cent of the respondents have told that they do not wish to continue study. Over 20 per cent of the respondents remained silent. 14 per cent of the respondents never thought of it. Most of the respondents are undertaking the household duties other than the outside work. Studying either in literacy classes or under regular stream would add to the burden the respondents already have. When they told that they don't want to study, they really meant that they do not want to take up additional burden in their busy life schedule.

Most of the families of the respondents are nuclear families. Most of the families are medium size with 4 – 6 members. Nearly one-third of the families are large families with more than 7 members. Joint families are mostly large size. Out of the 164 joint families only 6 are small size families. Average number of members per family is five.

3.9 per cent of the respondents who are unmarried have never thought of marriage. 2.3 per cent of the respondents seem to have the opinion not to get married as if they are being compelled to marry against their wish. 1.5 per cent of the respondents wish to live as housewives instead of remaining landless labour. It shows the wish of illiterate women to settle peacefully in life as housewives. Very few respondents are interested in securing a permanent job or saving money before getting married. Only a few unmarried respondents have realised the importance of economic independence before getting married. *Over 40 per cent of the respondents wish to educate their boys and prepare them for an alternate occupation.* 25 per cent of the respondents wish their children to be self-employed. 16.5 per cent of the respondents wish that their children would get a better wage while 7.6 per cent of the respondents wish to purchase land and work and see that their children would also work on that land. At least 23 per cent of the respondents have never thought of the future of their sons or have left the same in the hands of God. 31.5 per cent of the respondents have placed the highest priority on the marriage of their girl children. It seems that the most important concern for landless women labour is to get settled in marriage. Over 30 per cent of the respondents have either never thought of it or left it to the decision of God. *Barely 17 per cent of the respondents wish their girl children to study and 3 per cent of the respondents are concerned about the career of the girls.* The difference in the aspirations regarding the future plan for sons and daughters shows the gender discrimination practised in the families of landless women labour. *When their sons are oriented for a career in life, their daughters are oriented towards marriage.*

Majority of the respondents are politically active in the sense that they participate in election as voters. Almost 80 per cent of the respondents are interested in village level politics. The working class men as well as women were always the target group of various political parties. Unionism is very much common among agricultural labourers as in the case of industrial workers. The interest of political parties is limited in securing the vote of the landless labourers who are mostly illiterate. They seldom show interest in educating or improving the status of landless women labour. 80 per cent of the respondents have participated in the village level politics at various levels. Three respondents have contested the election. 19.2 per cent of the respondents have participated in political canvassing while as many as 80 per cent of the respondents have voted. The literacy rate of the respondents is as low as 15 per cent and their participation in political decision-making is very much limited. Their participation has ended with voting or canvassing. Their problems were never taken up by any political parties and their issues are hardly taken care of by any legislatures in India.

Economic and Occupational Profile

Economic and occupational profile of landless women labour refers to occupation of the respondents, income of the respondents, occupation of the head of the household, income of the family, actual income, per capita income, land owned, working conditions, work on land, period of employment, other activities of the LWL, kind of their work, involvement in household activities, expenditure of the respondents and what their husbands do with their income.

75 per cent of the heads of the household are engaged in unskilled or agricultural occupation. Only 6 per cent of the respondents are skilled labourers. 11.3 per cent of the heads of the family are hawkers or vendors. Occupationally the entire families of the respondents seem to be agricultural or unskilled daily labourers. Since majority of the landless labourers are illiterate they remain unskilled and are forced to look for unskilled agricultural occupations that yield poor income.

About 60 per cent of the respondents have disclosed their monthly income as below Rs. 2000 while over 60 per cent have the monthly income in between Rs. 2000 to Rs. 4000. Only 10 per cent of the respondents have their family income more than Rs. 4000 per month which means 90 per cent of the respondents have their annual income below Rs. 48,000. Over 30 per cent of the respondents have the per capita monthly income below Rs. 500 and 85 per cent of the respondents have the per capita income less than Rs. 1000. Only 15 per cent of the respondents have per capita income above Rs. 1000. It is also seen that smaller families have higher per capita income. Almost 50 per cent of the families with more than 7 members have the per capita income below Rs. 500. Out of 204 families with less than three members, only four families have the per capita income less than Rs. 500. Poor families are large families. The average size of the families below poverty line is above five. Illiterate parents are reluctant to adopt any family planning methods.

Only 7 per cent of the respondents have own land. Over 90 per cent of the respondents are landless. Those who are acquired land have acquired it recently by taking loans. Those who have land have relatively better family income.

At least 16.3 per cent of the respondents earn Rs. 500 or less per month and 44.8 per cent of the respondents earn between Rs. 500 to Rs. 1000 per month. 29.3 per cent of the respondents earn between Rs. 1000 to Rs. 1500 per month. Nearly 10 per cent of the respondents earn more than Rs. 1500 as personal income. Over 60 per cent of the respondents earn below Rs. 1000 per month which means below Rs. 40 per day. It is much below the minimum wage. Minimum wage for unskilled agricultural occupations in Delhi, U.P. and Haryana is between Rs. 70 to Rs. 110. Only 19 respondents secure minimum wages as per the government norms.

Less than 25 per cent of the respondents are working on the same piece of land for several generations. Over 60 per cent of the respondents do not work on the same piece of land for generations. 30 per cent of the respondents occupy others' land for more than 6 months a year while nearly 50 per cent of the respondents occupy others' land for three to six months. Nearly 20 per cent of the respondents occupy others' land for 30 days or less in a year. 70 per cent of the respondents work as landless labourers for less than six months in a year confirming a previous finding that the agricultural labour is only seasonal. This seasonal engagement does not satisfy the respondents and they are compelled to find some off-seasonal occupations.

Almost 60 per cent of the respondents do other activities to complement their seasonal agricultural occupation. Out of 464 respondents who are engaged in other activities, 228 respondents are engaged in agricultural occupations for 3 to 6 months, 190 are engaged in agricultural jobs in others' land for over 6 months. It is seen that among the respondents who are engaged in agricultural operation for less than 30 days a year, the majority are not engaged in other occupations. The need of the landless women labour is so pressing that they try to get any unskilled engagement to supplement their seasonal income.

Nearly 25 per cent of the respondents are working as construction workers during the off-seasons, and majority of them earn less than Rs. 1000 per month from such occupation. Over 20 per cent of the respondents are engaged in any unskilled daily labour available and there are no fixed occupations for them. Their monthly income is mostly between Rs. 500 to Rs. 1000. Nearly 10 per cent of the respondents have found off-seasonal occupation as domestic workers and most of them earn a monthly income more than Rs. 500. Only 5 per cent of the respondents are engaged in other off-seasonal occupations like handicrafts activities, work in the factories etc. Over 35 per cent of the respondents are not engaged in any alternate occupations in the off-seasons.

Majority of the respondents are engaged in construction works during the off-seasons. Agricultural operations are held mainly during the monsoon seasons and construction works are mainly done during the dry seasons. Monsoon is off-season for construction works. Much of the construction works are undertaken by the building contractors who recruit the easily available landless women labour as daily labours for the unskilled works. They seldom fight for the rights of a worker, such as minimum wage, workman's compensation, maternity leave, gratuity, increment, provident fund, ESI benefit etc. During the monsoon season these workers will go back to their respective villages to undertake the traditionally contracted agricultural works.

Apart from the seasonal agricultural works and off-seasonal supplementary works, the respondents have to discharge a number of household activities. 97.61 per cent of the respondents are doing the daily domestic routine like cooking, cleaning and washing. 62.83 per cent of the respondents have to look after the children, the elderly and the guests. 58.04 per cent of the respondents have to look after the cattle. Only 10.87 per cent of the respondents are engaged in some leisure time activities (hobbies) like stitching, knitting, singing, dancing and sitting with friends. Only 11 respondents spare time to supervise their children's home work. It is seen that only 2 respondents are studying and getting some vocational training in some non-agricultural trade.

Domestic responsibilities are inseparable routine of the rural women, whether they are working or non working. This is one of the reasons why rural women simply prefer to settle down in life as simple housewives. Housewives are undertaking silently the entire productive as well as non-productive but essential household responsibilities. In large size families, domestic duties like cleaning, cooking, washing, looking after the children and the elderly, fetching water and fuel, preparing 'Tiffin' for husband and children, and supervising the education of children alone consume the entire day time of the women.

About 84 per cent of the respondents spend their income in the family for food expenses. Landless women labour are leading a lifestyle of hand to mouth sustenance. Less than 1 per cent is spent for the education of the children, paying off the bank debts, and for savings. Nearly 10 per cent of the respondents do not have any fixed expenditure pattern. Much of their earnings are spent in their family for food. The families of landless women labour depend largely on the income of the women. The earnings of the respondents are very important for survival of their families. The work of female members is very important in poor families. Usually rural women are housewives. The poor illiterate women are happy to live like simple housewives. If they go out of home for any work, it is due to sheer necessity of survival. When their husbands are unable to earn enough to maintain the family, the rural women get out rendering a helping hand to them. They do these works not forgoing the domestic duties but after completing these works. Thus the burden of working women in rural areas is doubled.

It is a tradition in rural areas that the men hold property rights and the women have little share in the monetary affairs of the family. Usually the respondents hand over their earnings to their husbands. 41.6 per cent of the respondents believe that their husbands take the money and utilise it for meeting various expenses of the family. 34.4 per cent of the respondents have disclosed that their husbands have no concern with their earnings. 7 per cent of the respondents said that their husbands would save the money or entrust the same to themselves for saving. Only 6.4 per cent of the respondents have told that they do not know what their husbands would do with their earnings. All the respondents are very positive about the attitude of their husbands regarding the spending of their earnings. Combining this finding with the previous one, we can conclude that whether it is spent by the respondents or their husbands the purpose of the expenditure does not change. The lion's share is spent for the family and primarily to meet food expenses. What is spent on education, savings and other investments is very meagre.

Problems of Landless Women Labour (LWL)

The problems faced by landless women labour are multifarious. The most crucial problems faced by LWL are the harassment, wage differential and indebtedness. The disappointing aspect of the situation is that in most of the cases the victims of the social injustice are unable to react or get the assistance of legal machinery to reinstate justice. The situation is just accepted as normal both by the oppressors as well as the victims. Since no complaints are registered, the police is unable to intervene. For the victims, their fear of loss of livelihood prevents them from complaining against the landlords. Since these poor labourers are unskilled and therefore unable to look for any alternative occupation, they bear the harassment as part of their normal working condition. The anchor of indebtedness halts the landless women labour from taking bold decisions like changing the employer or migrating to far away places.

Only 12 respondents could emphatically say 'no' with regard to the incidence of workplace harassment. 35 per cent of the respondents have reported the incidence of workplace harassment and over 40 per cent of the respondents are not sure about the happenings of harassment or have not recognised certain behaviour as harassment. 40 per cent of the respondents have revealed the nature of harassment faced by them. 19.3 per cent of the respondents have disclosed that they feel insecure at the workplace due to harassment. 14.1 per cent of the respondents feel that the people are taking advantages all the time. Only 7.3 per cent of the respondents have reported good work atmosphere. All the incidents reported were the events of sexual harassment. 49.2 per cent of the respondents have not reported any incidents of workplace harassment.

About 65 per cent of the respondents have faced workplace harassment and 37.6 per cent of the respondents preferred to remain silent about it. Only 2.3 per cent of the respondents were ready to complain against the assailant to the Sarpancha or the Police. 21.9 per cent of the respondents disclosed the incidence to some elders or friends while 3.5 per cent of the respondents cursed the guilty and refused to disclose to anybody. Majority of the victims of social injustice remain silent. Either they are afraid of losing the job, or lost faith in the legal machinery, or don't wish to become notorious, or got used to and became insensitive to injustice. The primary objective of this study is to sensitise both the governmental and non-governmental agencies as well as the general public about the pathetic situation of the victims of social injustice, the landless women labour.

At least 12.39 per cent of the respondents are of the opinion that the Government should appoint some inspectors to check the incidence of workplace harassment or take some steps to punish the offenders to prevent the occurrence of workplace harassment. In vast majority of cases, the respondents are not aware of any role played by government in these situations. They blame themselves for not being careful enough to be victimised or remain silent. Lack of basic education and proper awareness regarding the existing legal machinery contribute to this situation. Government should take up some creative step in accordance with the recent Supreme Court guidelines regarding sexual harassment at workplace extending its scope to the unorganised agricultural sector.

Another serious problem faced by landless women labour is the prevalence of wage differential. 26 per cent of the respondents are clearly aware of the fact that they receive lower wages compared to their male counterpart. This awareness is a key factor for creative action. While we analyse the reaction we can see that very few dared to react. 37.6 per cent are not sure whether there is any difference in the wages between men and women. Many of the respondents in this category have their own justification for a higher wages for their male counter part. Only 15.9 per cent of the respondents receive equal wages for their work in comparison to their male counterpart.

At least 37.3 per cent of the respondents are aware of the fact that their wages are lower than that of their male counterpart. 14.1 per cent of the respondents have reported that their wages are 10 per cent less than that of their male counterpart. 5.6 per cent of the respondents have disclosed that their wages are ¾ or lesser compared to that of the male labourers. Nearly 8 per cent of the respondents are sure that their wages are lower but are not able to calculate it.

Nearly 6.4 per cent of the respondents were bold enough to ask the employer why there is difference in the wages between men and women. Over 36.3 per cent of the respondents either never thought of asking or were not confident enough to ask. What is revealed indirectly is that above 40 per cent of the respondents receive lower wages compared to their male counterpart. Majority of the respondents who experience wage differential do not ask for equal wages or don't bother about asking due to many reasons. They are either afraid of being punished or recognise for themselves the superiority of male labourers in all the situations both inside as well as outside home or are happy with what they get at present. Most of the respondents are not aware of their right for equal wages for equal work. Often women prefer peaceful negotiations at the workplace avoiding every chance of friction with male co-workers as well as male supervisors.

Only 10 per cent of the respondents received some answers for their query regarding the wage differential between male and female landless labourers. Among all the unreasonable responses the reference to the poor or lesser quality of women's work was the most frequent one, followed by the inferior quality of the overall performance of women and the inferior quality of women's work. The inability of women to undertake certain operations was the rarest response. Since 85 per cent of the respondents were illiterate, the employers could easily satisfy them with irrational answers. The reasons given by the employers confirm the prevailing stereotypes regarding the women's work. These explanations have simply reinforced the false self image of the respondents who silently bore the injustice done against them. Illiterate and ignorant women are thus victimised. Unless organised efforts are undertaken to impart literacy and basic education victims of social injustice cannot be helped in any way.

At least 24 respondents discussed the matter with the family members. All these respondents could not dare to ask the employer. 48 respondents were daring to ask the employer why they were paid less. While most of the respondents remained inactive with regard to less wages paid to them. Those who asked were sent back with unreasonable answers. None could take up any effective step with regard to fewer wage paid to them.

Rural indebtedness is the most common problem of the landless labourers. 166 respondents have taken loan and another 18 women have taken some borrowings which they are not sure whether they are debt in real sense or not. Families with lower income have incurred debt and their ability to repay the same is very much limited. 23.7 per cent of the respondents have taken loan and 10.43 per cent of the respondents have taken loan to purchase land which is a progressive trend. Another 9.78 per cent of the respondents have taken loan for meeting the expenses of marriage. Less than 4 per cent of the respondents have incurred debt for other purposes like house construction, purchase of cattle, medical care, and to clear off old debts.

The respondents have taken loan for meeting the expenses of the marriage mostly from their employer, between Rs. 10,000 to 15,000 for a period less than one year and for less than 4 per cent interest per month. It is also seen that most of these loans are not returned. The respondents have taken loan for purchase of land mostly from the money lenders, between Rs. 15,000 to 20,000 for a period more than one year and for 4 - 8 per cent interest per month. It is seen that most of these loans are being returned. The most popular source of loan is money-lenders, the respondents take on an average of Rs. 10,000 to 20,000 as loans, for a period of one to three years, at the rate of 4 to 8 per cent per month and majority of them are returning or have returned the loan.

Role of Governmental and Non-Governmental Agencies

The illiterate landless women labours are found to be ignorant about various government efforts to emancipate them. Therefore, the participation of these people is also very meagre. 70 per cent of the respondents are of the opinion that reservation for women in various fields is very useful. Reservation in legislative bodies, job scenario, educational and vocational institutions would bring out a desirable development in the status of women. Reservation is an effective strategy to ensure the participation of women in political, economic and social fields of life. Due to the practice of age old patriarchal values, women are systematically kept away from the decision-making bodies at political and economic fields. Managerial level positions in the industrial and service sectors are often not accessible to women. Only a carefully formulated reservation policy would ensure a decent participation of women in every walk of life.

At least 5.9 per cent of the respondents are of the opinion that the welfare schemes of government can improve the lives of women. Majority of the respondents are suspicious about the benefit of welfare schemes in their lives. What is required at this moment is to find ways and means to secure the faith of women in the utility of welfare schemes of government. If the respondents approach the welfare schemes with negative attitudes and prejudice they will not be able to get any benefit out of the schemes. Over the years the government agencies have presented themselves as the friends of the employers who are better educated and influential. It is quite natural that the educated citizens have greater access to the welfare schemes and various other services offered by the governmental agencies. The illiterate people tend to believe that the government departments are set up for serving the well off citizens who use various laws and other service delivery systems to suppress the marginalised. Public servants are in an urgent need to get sensitised towards the needs of the landless women labour who are illiterate and vulnerable. Once the governmental agencies have proved themselves trustworthy, the poor people will boldly approach them for assistance. Unless and until such an attitudinal change is induced among the respondents, no government schemes seem to bring out desirable impact in the lives of landless women labour.

Only 8.05 per cent of the respondents have heard about various government schemes for rural development. A vast majority of the respondents are not aware of any government schemes for rural development and practically none of them have ever benefited from such schemes. Among the few schemes, known to the respondents, Balika Samridhi Yojana and Jawahar Gram Samridhi Yojana are more popular than other schemes. Governmental agencies must give a serious thought about this finding. What the investigator feels is that the procedure of implementation of government schemes should be friendlier to the illiterate people. The illiterate women are often scared of approaching any governmental agencies for any help. Mass education strategies especially the literacy education is a pre-condition for the success of any scheme designed for the welfare of the landless women labour. Often the schemes are not addressed to the target groups in the form of strategies meeting their felt needs. The primary need of the landless women labour as reflected in this study is the need for land ownership.

About 75 per cent of the respondents want the government to allot some land for cultivation at a subsidised price. Over 50 per cent of the respondents wish that the government might open up more employment opportunities in the government departments or reserve more jobs for the landless women labour. 26 per cent of the respondents were of the opinion that government should create greater opportunities for education and training of landless women labour. Other expectations of the respondents from the government include provision of community health services, allotment of house sites, electricity, widow pensions etc. Preference is given to the acquisition of land. This discloses the value placed by the respondents in agriculture and cultivable land. For the landless women labour land is still considered as the most useful and valuable productive resource and want the government to create provision for redistribution of land. This shows that the respondents regard agricultural works as the essential means for livelihood. Keeping this as the first preference the respondents have asked for alternative employment opportunities in service sector or industrial sector. Even if the respondents are mostly illiterate, they look for alternate occupations, often as a substitute or an alternate for their first preference of land. This finding shows again the general belief that the illiterate mass considers land as the most valuable resource and they regard physical exertion or labour intensive agricultural operations as the primary means for living.

Only 3 respondents seem to have heard about any NGOs working for them. No respondents seem to believe in the role of NGOs in improving their lives. This finding points to the fact that very few NGOs are working for the welfare of the landless women labour. The respondents belong to the marginalised section of the society who are not taken care of both by governmental and the non-governmental agencies. Several reasons can be assigned to this situation. Since the landless women labourers are engaged almost all the days in a week in work they are scarcely available to the access of any NGOs. Since these people are overburdened with both the household and the outside occupations, they seldom find time and convenience to attend any meeting held by NGOs. Another reason could be that most of the respondents are illiterate and they do not read any letters or notice served to them by NGOs. This finding is a reminder for NGOs in the field of rural development regarding the effectiveness of their programmes and activities. They should find out innovative strategies to approach this marginalised section of the society. Carefully planned programmes are to be formulated to uplift landless women labour. These women expect both governmental and non-governmental agencies to work for asserting their rights for cultivable land.

Matters arising out of findings

- Majority of the respondents are below 35 years of age.
- Most of the respondents are married. None remain unmarried after the age of 25.
- A vast majority of the landless women labour belong to the backward or scheduled caste and the scheduled tribes.

- Majority of the respondents are illiterate. The younger generation is better educated.
- Parents prefer to educate the boy children and send the girls for work in the field.
- Most of the respondents have their monthly income below Rs. 2000. Most of the respondents have their annual income below Rs. 48,000.
- Majority of the respondents have the per capita income less than Rs. 1000 which means below Rs. 40 per day much below minimum wages.
- Poor families are large families. The average size of the families below poverty line is above five.
- Majority of the landless women labour do work for less than six months a year. Majority of the respondents do other activities to complement their seasonal agricultural occupation.
- Majority of the respondents are engaged in construction works during the off seasons.
- Domestic responsibilities are inseparable routine of the rural women, whether they are working or non-working. This is one of the reasons why rural women simply prefer to settle down in life as simple housewives.
- The families of landless women labour depend largely on the income of the women. The earnings of the respondents are very important for survival of their families. The work of female members is very important in poor families.
- The lion's share is spent for the family and primarily for food expenses.
- The problems faced by landless women labour are multifarious. The most crucial problems faced by LWL are the harassment, wage differential and indebtedness.
- Most of the respondents have faced workplace harassment.
- All the incidents reported were the events of sexual harassment. Majority of the victims of social injustice remain silent.
- Majority of the respondents who experience wage

differential do not ask for equal wages or don't bother about asking. Most of the respondents are not aware of their right for equal wages for equal work.

- Majority of the respondents are suspicious about the benefit of welfare schemes in their lives. Only a few respondents have heard about various government schemes for rural development. A vast majority of the respondents are not aware of any government schemes for rural development and practically none of them have ever benefited from such schemes.
- The primary need of the landless women labour as reflected in this study is the need for land ownership. Majority of the respondents want the government to allot some land for cultivation at a subsidised price.
- Other expectations of the respondents from the government include opportunities for employment in the government, reserve more jobs, create opportunities for education and training of landless women labour, provision of community health services, allotment of house sites, electricity, widow pensions etc.
- Hardly anyone has heard about any NGOs working for them. No respondents seem to believe in the role of NGOs in improving their lives.
- The landless women labours expect both governmental and non-governmental agencies to work for asserting their rights for cultivable land.

Conclusions

This study has realised all the objectives set before the study.

- This study has been a successful attempt to understand the magnitude and intensity of the problem concerning landless women labour in the States of Delhi, U.P. and Haryana.
- It has studied the respondents' desires, vision and aspirations for themselves and for their children.

- The study has found out the impact of governmental and non-governmental welfare activities on the landless women labourers.
- It has also examined the role of various socio-political institutions in their lives.
- This study has also attempted to analyse the specific problems of minorities, SC and ST groups of women who are working as landless labourers.
- Finally the study has suggested some measures which can bring about some improvement in their life style, mental make up and socio-economic situation of landless women labourers.

Suggestions and Recommendations:

- ***For the Government***: Governmental efforts for the welfare of the landless women labourers and other marginalised sections of the society are not properly propagated to the beneficiaries. Mass communication strategies such as, advertisement through Doordarshan and Akashvani, propagation in schools, announcements at railway stations, announcement at public gatherings of political parties, advertisement through posters and banners at public places such as bus stands and hospitals, are to be adopted for the effective development communication.
- Land should be redistributed among the landless labourers. Government should reclaim the waste lands and provide land rights to the landless labourers. This would put an end to the nomadic life style of the landless women labour.
- Cells should be created to prevent work place harassment. The illiterate women labourers are easy victims of work place harassment and the crime intervention cells must take an active role in preventing work place harassment in the rural areas.
- Government should implement the labour laws strictly. Land laws and the labour laws are recently amended in

favour of casual labourers and the benefits are yet to reach the landless women labour.

- As part of rural development programmes, Self-Help Group movement is on in the countryside. Government grants and subsidies are available to the groups of women of below poverty line. Landless women labour are not able to avail any benefits under the scheme. Government must relax the conditions to extend the benefits to the groups of landless women labour.
- Vocational training programmes should be planned for the landless women labour. Government must introduce stipends and grants for these women to attend the programmes.
- Illiteracy being the first diagnosed social evil among the landless women labour is to be effectively addressed by the government in the rural areas of U.P. and Haryana.
- Reimbursement strategy is to be adopted for the implementation of educational and vocational scholarship schemes for the economically and socially backward sections of the society including the landless women labour.
- Gender sensitisation is to be imparted at the grass-root level to the agricultural households, students of high school and higher secondary level, agricultural workers, their supervisory staff, professional groups such as teachers, lawyers, nurses, doctors, political and administrative personalities by means of group dynamic sessions, participatory learning methods, street plays, leadership training of women's groups (Self-Help Groups), and by means of many other groups interaction methods. More and more men are to be encouraged to participate in gender sensitisation programmes, so that they will be sensitive towards the rights of women and their needs for equality and empowerment.
- Legal and executive machinery of the State are to be gender sensitive. They must recognise the equality of women in every walk of life, enforce the protective and preventive

strategy to safeguard the rights of women, enforce stringent measures to control abuse and violence against women, act promptly and positively to prevent exploitation and harassment at workplace, and cooperate with different organisations working for women empowerment.

- Training for capacity building and assertiveness is to be imparted to girl students at high school and higher secondary level, so that they will assert their rights in various social situation, disclose the episodes of harassment and exploitation at home and workplace, approach legal and police aid fearlessly, remind the male supervisors regarding their rights and extend support to the co-students and co-workers in need.
- Equal opportunity for every job should be given to women. Reservation for women in I and II class government jobs is to be enhanced to ensure 50 per cent participation of women in key bureaucratic positions in the state. Effective provisions are to be devised to check workplace harassment. Maternity leave must be enforced in every category of occupations both in organised and unorganised sectors. Equality of wages, equality of work load, equality in the provision of promotion and equal participation in management and decision-making of the industry for the women employees are to be ensured. Gender sensitisation of male co-workers and male supervisors is to be carried out so that they would recognise and respect the rights of women for justice and equality. Omission of query regarding the gender of the applicant for any job, equal treatment of both men and women at every stage of pre-service and in-service training, giving opportunity for women professionals to take decisions and execute them, and above all bring up hope and self-confidence among girls and women regarding their capacity to undertake any profession, trade or service that men take up are other measures to empower marginalised women.
- At the level of political organisation, equal opportunity

must be provided for women to participate actively in political parties, to deliver political speech, to organise political gatherings, to express public will at public platforms, to head petitioners in civil offices, to campaign for elections, to contest election, to hold ministerial positions, to head various legislative committees, to lead the opposition, to head the state, to govern the state, to hold judicial positions, to hold important positions in the Army, Navy and Air Force and above all recognise the rights of women to partake the destiny of our nation on equal basis with that of men. 50 per cent reservation for women in the legislative, judicial and executive positions is a must for ensuring equal participation of women in the political destiny of the nation. She must have equal share in every decision taken in the nation at any level of political organisation from local to international which affect the destiny of both men and women equally. It is unfair that men take the political decisions and the women remain just as the beneficiary or the subjects of those decisions. It is time to recognise and respect the right of women to take responsibility for her destiny.

- ***For the Educational Planners:*** Girls and boys should be treated equal. Equal opportunities are to be given in every educational stream. Home science should be a compulsory subject at high school level for both boys and girls. Literature involving the subjugation of women in the curricula must be replaced by literature highlighting equality and empowerment of women. Lessons of history must include the stories of eminent women of the history. Equal career orientation must be imparted in the schools. Girls' right for education of their choice must be respected. Girls must be encouraged to continue their education after marriage. Reservation for girls at the level of professional education must be introduced to bridge the present shortage in the representation of women professionals and above all the right of girls for self-realisation in education must be respected. Eradication of illiteracy being the felt need of the landless women labour must systematically be addressed by educational institutions in the rural areas.

- ***For the Village Panchayats:*** Village Panchayats must take creative steps to mitigate the problems of the landless women labour. Since the 73rd Amendment of the Constitution (1993), Panchayats are given more powers and development funds. The landless women labour must be included in various schemes of the Panchayats.
- ***For the Civil Society*:** Women must have equal opportunity for participation in every social function. Discrimination based on gender must be systematically eliminated in religious functions, cultural activities and community festivals. Equality and autonomy in the choice of dress code, wearing or not wearing ornaments, freedom and autonomy upon her own body and life, right to limit child birth, freedom to exercise the rights for moving or not moving out of house for attending public functions, right to pursue any hobby, right to observe or not to observe *Purdah*, right to hold property, right to save, invest or spend money for meeting personal needs without consulting with men of the household, freedom to consume economic resources for her welfare, right to demand equal participation of men of the household in the domestic duties of child rearing, cooking, cleaning and washing, and above all the right to resist social pressure to uphold the traditional stereotype of 'womanhood' are the rights be recognised and respected to ensure women's empowerment.
- Women must recognise for themselves, their right for equality of opportunities with men in every walk of life; they must realise the areas of their strengths and weakness, areas of threats and opportunities; they must take responsibility for themselves regarding their life and career; take responsibility of the results of the decisions taken by them; take enough precautions and preventive measures to protect themselves in odd circumstances; realise for themselves the need for economic self support, equality in

political leadership, and right for equal opportunity in education, vocational training and preparation for any trade, service and profession; they must respect their own body and life and nurture a sense of dignity and self esteem that would enable them to resist any attempt to enslave their life and liberty before any men; and above all, women should learn to realise for themselves the essential equality of the human endowment embodied in their body which is in no way inferior to the endowment in the body of men.

Long Term Measures to Improve the Status of Landless Women Labour

- ***Improve the barren land:*** The improvement of the cultivated landscape would provide employment for the landless women labour all through out the year and their term of employment would thus become permanent. The procurement of permanent labour gives her rights of workmen and the social security provisions will be applicable to them.
- ***Development of country side:*** Infra-structural development of the rural areas would provide opportunities for the landless women labour to improve their living. More roads, provision for drinking water, electricity, provision for school and hospital facilities would prevent migration of rural labourers to cities during the dry seasons. Infra-structural development of the country side would promote the growth of small scale and cottage industries providing supplementary sources of income to the marginal and landless labourers.
- ***Other Long-term measures:*** Education, general uplift of socio economic condition of the rural poor, proper implementation of land laws and the labour laws.

Summing up

In the final analysis we can conlude that the plight of women landless labour is unlimited. It is not easy to control or curb this problem unless a massive programme is chalked out, resources are upgraded and alternative arrangements are made for rendering the services which women landless labour are doing on meagre wages. Besides, any solution for the problems of women landless labour needs dedicated workers, faultless plan, complete involvement of the civil society and a true political will.

However, this grim situation should not stop us from working. Whatever little is possible should be initiated. We should understand that the torch bearers in this crusade are NGOs. As member of the civil society we should stop looking towards the government for solving every issue.

Suggestions given in the above line are simple and practical, they do not promise an entry into a utopian world, rather they would take us one step forward.

Annexure-1

UN CHARTER OF DEMANDS OF LANDLESS WOMEN

This Charter of demands was adopted by more than 3000 landless delegates from communities across South Africa and their landless allies from across the world at the Landless People's Assembly held in Durban on 30 August, 2001— the Day of the Landless at the 3rd United Nations World Conference against Racism— as an initiative of the Landless People's Movement.

"We, the landless people of South Africa, declare our needs for our government and the world to know.

We are the people who have borne the brunt of colonialism and neo-colonialism, of the invasion of our land by the wealthy countries of the world, of the theft of our natural resources, and of forced labour for the colonists.

We are the people who have borne the brunt of apartheid, of forced removals from our fields and homes, of poverty in the rural areas, of oppression on the farms and of starvation, neglect and disease in the Bantustans. We have suffered from migrant labour, which has caused our family life and communities to collapse. We have starved because of unemployment and low wages. We have seen our children stunted because of little food, no water and no sanitation. We have seen our land dry up and blow away in the wind, because we have been forced into smaller and smaller places.

We continue to suffer under these conditions because the legacy of colonialism and apartheid has not been defeated in our areas. We continue to suffer from forced removals from our homes, from evictions — legal and illegal— from the farms we have worked for generations, and from gross violations of our basic human rights through abuse at the hands of the farmers who own these lands. We continue to suffer widespread injustices due to the racist criminal justice system in our areas that will not support us. We are the people who still bear the brunt of this legacy and the neo-liberal policies which today require us to buy back our stolen land and pay for services we have never enjoyed, while taking away our jobs and driving our young people into the cities. These are the biggest problems facing our country today.

We fought for the end of colonialism and apartheid, and welcomed the birth of a new South Africa. But for us there is nothing new because there is still no land, no services and no growth in our areas. We will no longer sit back and watch as the wealth builds up in the hands of a tiny urban elite, while on the edges of the cities, in the small towns and in the countryside, we continue to suffer and starve.

These are our demands. We have discussed them in each of our communities, in our regions and as a nation of landless people.

Noting that

Almost 350 years have passed since the first colonists arrived on our shores to force us off our land;

Since that time, colonialism and apartheid brutally and systematically dispossessed our people of most of the land of South Africa, leaving the African population on 13 per cent of the land, with the remaining 87 per cent of land held by white farmers and the state;

Our ancestors fought for all of that time to keep their land, and we placed our hopes for the return of our birthright in the liberation movement that we supported and helped to put in power;

Land reform, including restitution, redistribution and tenure reform, were promised to us as the country's landless people in 1994, and are required by the Constitution for which we fought;

The Reconstruction and Development Programme promised to redistribute 30 per cent of agricultural land between 1994 and 1999, but today less than 2 per cent of land— mostly poor quality —has been redistributed through land reform;

The restitution programme has delivered very little land reform due to the slow processing of claims;

The redistribution programme, which has moved even more slowly, has not allowed people who qualify for housing grants to obtain land, causing great hardship to landless people, especially children and labour tenants, who need land for livestock grazing and crops;

The new Land Redistribution for Agricultural Development (LRAD) programme does not offer a solution, because it also does not recognise that as landless people, we need land for many different things;

The tenure reform programme has delivered nothing to our people because most of our people still do not have formal land rights and cannot invest in our land;

Our people who have received land have been unable to use it effectively due to a lack of post-settlement support;

Our people who work on farms constantly have their basic human rights violated through abuse, evictions, slave-like working conditions and racism;

Our children who live on farms are forced to labour on them and suffer from a lack of schooling facilities;

Our people cannot receive justice due to biased and racist police and magistrates in rural areas;

The World Bank's "market-led, willing seller-willing buyer" land reform formula has failed in Zimbabwe and many other countries, and is failing and will continue to fail in South Africa;

Poverty remains greatest in the rural areas, where 70 per cent of South Africa's poor live, including a disproportionate number of women, children and elderly people, yet rural development receives lower priority than urban development;

We continue to live as exiles in the land of our birth, denied the basic attributes of citizenship through subjection to abuse and exploitation at the hands of those who benefited from apartheid and who still own most of the land;

Although there are many policies and laws in place, there has been very little improvement in our lives;

We still lack the most basic services and infrastructure;

Our taxes and national resources are being used to repay apartheid debts and buy expensive weapons rather than to develop our country and our people;

We are no longer consulted about the policies that are supposed to transform our lives; and inspite of the slow delivery of land reform, our people have received little communication and report-backs from the government.

And Putting on Record that

We, the landless people of South Africa have not sat idly by waiting for the government to deliver our land to us;

We have adopted the Community Land Charter in 1994 on the eve of the new South Africa, and waited patiently for the new government to deliver the land reform it promised to us;

We have adopted the Rural People's Charter in 1999 and tried to influence the policies that affect us;

We have written letters to request meetings with the Minister of Agriculture and Land Affairs and the President;

Due to the lack of response to such letters, we have organised numerous pickets and submitted various memoranda to the President;

We have submitted various other memoranda to relevant national and provincial government departments;

We have held provincial land rights conferences and submitted the resolutions of these conferences to our provincial governments;

We have held regional conferences to strengthen regional land reform forums comprising landless communities within our regions; however, our efforts have not resulted in sufficient responsiveness from the government, nor in any significant change to the problems of land reform; We are still waiting for our land.

We therefore Demand : Land

"The land that was stolen from us must be returned! Give us our land now".

(1) We need our land to live on, for grazing, farming, economic opportunities and community facilities.
(2) The colonial and apartheid landscape on which white people own most of the land must be radically altered so that land is shared proportionately between blacks and whites. We say, "One farmer, one farm!"
(3) The RDP target of redistributing 30 per cent of land must be delivered immediately, as this is merely a first installment on the equitable redistribution that must finally be achieved.
(4) Land reform must be implemented rapidly and comprehensively.
(5) Outstanding land restitution cases must be urgently finalised.
(6) Land tenure reform must be implemented urgently, especially in the former Bantustans.
(7) The market-led, willing seller-willing buyer, demand-driven land reform programme must be scrapped and replaced with a state-led, needs-based, supply-led programme.
(8) People who have been evicted from their land, farm dwellers and other poor landless people should be given top priority for land reform.
(9) Government resettlement programmes must provide for the different land needs of communities. Not all rural people want to farm, but all rural people need land.
(10) Government must provide adequate support to people who acquire land through land reform to enable them to make the land productive and liveable.
(11) Communities already living on trust land or government land must be given the title deeds to the land.
(12) Communities who were forcibly removed from their land through colonialism and apartheid must have their land and mineral rights returned immediately and unconditionally.
(13) Land restoration should take precedence over financial

compensation in the restitution programme, so that land begins to shift from white to black ownership.

(14) The bulk of the land restitution budget should be spent supporting claimant communities to make their land productive, rather than paying huge compensation to the beneficiaries of apartheid.

(15) Indigenous peoples' right to the land must be recognised. Communities must be able to make claims to land that were taken from them as far back as 1652.

(16) Communities should be compensated for damages and losses suffered due to their forced removal.

(17) When land is restored to a community, it must be shared fairly within a community. There must be no discrimination as to who has access to land - especially not against women.

(18) All black people in South Africa who need land must have a right to land reform, because we all lost land through colonialism and apartheid.

(19) All vacant state land held by the national, provincial and municipal governments must be urgently transferred at no cost to poor landless communities.

(20) The state must become an active player in the land market, making land available for land reform through a supply-led land reform programme.

(21) The land that is chosen for redistribution must be fertile and we must be able to use it productively.

(22) All unproductive, unused, vacant or indebted private land should be targeted for redistribution to poor landless people.

(23) A social obligations clause must be added to our Constitution so that landless people can legally take action through self-reliance to take over unproductive land and make it productive, pending supplementary legal recognition.

(24) A land ceiling and land tax should be imposed to reduce large white landholdings.

(25) The government must actively utilise its powers to expropriate land for land reform.

(26) No landowner should be allowed to hold land reform to ransom to demand huge compensation.
(27) The compensation formula paid to existing landowners should be based on the productive value of the land, less apartheid state benefits received.
(28) The government must make land reform a priority and should allocate at least 10 per cent of its annual budget to bring about rapid land reform.
(29) Government must scrap the property rights clause and replace it with a "social obligations" clause imposing a "use-it-or-lose-it" condition on land ownership to make land that is under-utilised, unused or unproductive, or owned by absentee landlords available for land reform, and to enable landless people to bring about productive land reform through their own self-reliance, rather than forcing us to wait another seven years for the bureaucracy to complete its paperwork.
(30) Government must call a Land Summit by October 2001 to review the land reform programme.

Farm Dwellers

"We, the farm workers and labour tenants, demand access to land and security of tenure. Laws and practices which victimise us must be scrapped, and institutions which fail to serve our needs must be transformed":

1. Farm workers and labour tenants should be given land of their own.
2. The government must declare a moratorium on all evictions until a new law is adopted to protect farm dwellers.
3. Farm owners who abuse and exploit their workers must be prosecuted and must forfeit their land for land reform.
4. We demand a halt to all evictions of labour tenants and farm workers. The Extension of Security of Tenure Act and the Land Reform (Labour Tenants) Act must be amended to stop evictions and give farm dweller real land rights. We want legal protection and security of tenure.

5. We should not lose our homes if we do not continue working on the farm, or if we are disabled or pensioned. The wives and widows of farm workers must not be thrown off the land because of the circumstances of their husbands.
6. Laws must be passed to protect people working on farms from abuse and exploitation. These laws must include minimum wages. Firm steps must be taken to oversee that labour laws on farms are implemented.
7. Farm workers must be informed of their new rights, and provided with adequate legal support to enforce them. Farm workers should also be involved in making laws.
8. Farm workers should be paid the same rates as other workers in towns because they work equally hard.
9. Women farm workers should be paid the same as men.
10. A fair share of the rural policing budget should be spent protecting our rights.
11. Rural police, magistrates and prosecutors who fail to protect our rights must be fired and prosecuted.
12. Farm workers and tenants must be given secure rights to plough and graze their cattle. These rights should be protected when a farm changes hands.
13. Farmers must be responsible for supporting orphaned children of deceased workers.
14. We want an end to child labour on farms. People breaking this law must be monitored and severely punished.
15. Farm evictees, tenants and other landless people should be given top priority in any land reform programme.
16. Groups who can service and assist farm dwellers should immediately have free access to the farms. Farm worker unions should be legally entitled to organise workers on farms.
17. Special pieces of land should be set aside for farm workers villages.
18. We must be able to bury our loved ones on the farms where we live.
19. The government should take ownership of portions of land

on farms for the use of the people living on the farms. This land can be used for schools, sports fields and clinics, for example, which must be owned and run by the state instead of the farmers.

20. Farm workers must be provided with safe transportation to and from towns.
21. Farmers must not be allowed to employ immigrant workers on three-month contracts, and the rights of immigrant workers should be protected to prevent use of immigrant labour from undermining farm workers' rights and wage levels.

Women

"Women must be able to own land, and have equal rights in all areas of their lives".

1. Women should be able to own land whether they are married or single. Women and men should have the same rights to land. Married couples should have their houses registered in the names of both spouses.
2. Women should have equal representation on local government and other decision-making structures affecting their lives, including traditional authorities.
3. There should be no discrimination against women in inheritance rights.
4. Women should benefit from development programmes and be targeted for training. There should be special training centres and adult education courses geared for women.
5. Women living on farms must have secure places to live.
6. There should be special housing subsidies for women who cannot afford to buy houses or pay rent. Housing subsidies must be introduced to assist women who are single parents.
7. Land should be set aside for community facilities that benefit women, such as crèches, community gardens and women's training centres.

8. Women and children must have places to go if they are abused.
9. Rural development plans, especially job creation and skills development programmes, must prioritise the needs of women and must include adequate means of monitoring their actual impact on women.
10. The quota system of affirmative action should be imposed in tribal authorities and other rural structures, and tribal laws and practice that oppress rural women should be reviewed.

Beyond Land

"There must be democratic, non-racial, non-sexist local government in all our communities."
"There must be affordable houses for all."
"There must be affordable services for all our people."
"There must be participatory rural development."
"Our environment must be protected and used in a sustainable way."

The Way Forward

"Landless people must organise or starve".

1. We, as the landless people of South Africa, must get organised.
2. We must form local structures in all our communities to take forward our demands.
3. We must build unity in our communities to strengthen our hand in negotiations.
4. We, as the farm workers of South Africa, must get organised.
5. We, as the landless women of South Africa, must build women's forums in our regions to discuss land, and organise ourselves at a local and regional level to make sure our concerns are addressed.

6. We must build the Landless People's Movement to ensure that our voices are heard and our demands met.
7. We must build solidarity with other landless people throughout the world.
8. We must send a memorandum from this conference to the present government to make sure they know what our demands are.
9. We must organise local and regional actions to support our demands.
10. If our demands are not met, we will launch a campaign to occupy vacant land and state land, and return to our land.

These demands we will fight for, side by side throughout our lives, until we have won our land.

A World Conference against Racism Campaign by

The Landless People's Movement (LPM), The National Land Committee (NLC), The Rural Development Services Network (RDSN), The South African Ngo Coalition (SANGOCO).

Annexure-2

BONDED LABOUR SYSTEM (ABOLITION) ACT, 1976

(ACT NO. 19 OF 1976)

Preamble

[Act 19 of 1976 as amended by Act 73 of 1985]

[9th February, 1976]

An Act to provide for the abolition of bonded labour system with a view to preventing the economic and physical exploitation of the weaker sections of the people and for matters connected therewith or incidental thereto. Be it enacted by Parliament in the Twenty-seventh Year of the Republic of India as follows :

1. Short Title, Extent and Commencement

(1) This Act may be called the Bonded Labour System (Abolition) Act, 1976.
(2) It extends to the whole of India.
(3) It shall be deemed to have come into force on the 25th day of October, 1975.

2. Definitions

In this Act, unless the context otherwise requires,—

(a) "advance" means an advance, whether in cash or kind, or partly in cash or partly in kind, made by one person (hereinafter referred to as the creditor) to another person (hereinafter referred to as the debtor);

(b) "agreement" means an agreement (whether written or oral, or partly written and partly oral) between a debtor and creditor, and includes an agreement providing for forced labour, the existence of which is presumed under any social custom prevailing in the concerned locality.

Explanation : The existence of an agreement between the debtor and creditor is ordinarily presumed, under the social customs, in relation to the following forms of forced labour, namely : *Adiyamar, Baramasia, Basahya, Bethu, Bhagela, Cherumar, Garru- Galu, Hali, Hari, Harwail, Holya, Jana, Jeetha, Kamiya, Khundit- Mundit, Kuthia, Lakhari, Munjhi, Mat, Munish system, Nit-Majoor, Paleru, Padiyal, Pannayilal, Sagri, Sanji, Sanjawat, Sewak, Sewakia, Seri, Vetti;*

(c) "ascendant" or "descendant", in relation to a person belonging to a matriarchal society, means the person who corresponds to such expression in accordance with the law of succession in force in such society;

(d) "bonded debt" means an advance obtained, or presumed to have been obtained, by a bonded labourer under, or in pursuance of, the bonded labour system;

(e) "bonded labour" means any labour or service rendered under the bonded labour system;

(f) "bonded labourer" means a labourer who incurs, or has, or is presumed to have, incurred, a bonded debt;

(g) "bonded labour system" means the system of forced, or partly forced, labour under which a debtor enters, or has, or is presumed to have, entered, into an agreement with the creditor to the effect that —

(i) in consideration of an advance obtained by him or by any of his lineal ascendants or descendants (whether or not such advance is evidenced by the document) and in consideration of the interest, if any, due on such advance, or

(ii) in pursuance of any customary or social obligation, or

(iii) in pursuance of any obligation devolving on him by succession, or

(iv) for any economic consideration received by him or by any of his lineal ascendants or descendants, or

(v) by reason of his birth in any particular caste or community, he would—

(1) render, by himself or through any member of his family, or any person dependent on him, labour or service, to the creditor, or for the benefit of the creditor, for a specific period or for an unspecified period, either without wages or for nominal wages, or

(2) forfeit the freedom of employment or other means of livelihood for an specified period or for an unspecified period, or

(3) forfeit the right to move freely throughout the territory of India, or

(4) forfeit the right to appropriate or sell at market-value any of his property or product of his labour or the labour of a member of his family or any person dependent on him and includes the system of forced; or partly forced, labour under which a surety for a debtor enters, or has, or is presumed to have, entered into an agreement with the creditor to the effect that in the event of the failure of the debtor to repay the debt, he would render the bonded labour on behalf of the debtor;

Explanation : For the removal of doubts, it is hereby declared that any system of forced, or partly forced labour under which any workman being contract labour as defined in clause (b) of sub-section (1) of Section 2 of the Contract Labour (Regulation and Abolition) Act, 1970 (37 of 1970), or an Inter-State Migrant Workman as defined in clause (e) of sub-section (1) of Section 2 of the Inter-State Migrant Workman (Regulation of Employment and Conditions of Service) Act, 1979 (30 of 1979), is required to render labour or service in circumstances of the nature mentioned in sub-clause (1) of this clause or is subjected to all or any of the disabilities referred to in sub-clauses (2) to (4), is 'bonded labour system' within the meaning of this clause.

(h) "family", in relation to a person, includes the ascendant and descendant of such person;

(i) "nominal wages", in relation to any labour, means a wage which is less than,—

(a) the minimum wages fixed by the Government, in relation to the same or similar labour, under any law for the time being in force ; and

(b) where no such minimum wage has been fixed in relation to any form of labour, the wages that are normally paid, for the same or similar labour, to the labourers working in the same locality;

(j) "prescribed" means prescribed by rules made under this Act.

3. Act to have Overriding Effect

The provisions of this Act shall have effect notwithstanding anything inconsistent therewith contained in any enactment other than this Act, or in any instrument having effect by virtue of any enactment other than this Act.

4. Abolition of Bonded Labour System

(1) On the commencement of this Act, the bonded labour system shall stand abolished and every bonded labourer

shall, on such commencement, stand freed and discharged from any obligation to render, any bonded labour.

(2) After the commencement of this Act, no person shall—
   (a) make any advance under, or in pursuance of, the bonded labour system, or
   (b) compel any person to render any bonded labour or other form of forced labour.

5. Agreement, Custom etc., to be Void

On the commencement of this Act, any custom or tradition or any contract, agreement or other instrument (whether entered into or executed before or after the commencement of this Act,) by virtue of which any person, or any member of the family or dependent of such person, is required to do any work or render any service as a bonded labourer, shall be void and inoperative.

6. Liability to Repay Bonded Debt to Stand Extinguished

(1) On the commencement of this Act, every obligation of a bonded labourer to repay any bonded debt, or such part of any bonded debt unsatisfied immediately before such commencement, shall be deemed to have been extinguished.
(2) After the commencement of this Act, no suit or other proceedings shall lie in any civil or before any other authority for the recovery of any bonded debt or any part thereof.
(3) Every decree or order for the recovery of bonded debt, passed before the commencement of this Act and not fully satisfied before such commencement, shall be deemed, on such commencement, to have been fully satisfied.
(4) Every attachment made before the commencement of this Act, for the recovery of any bonded debt, shall, on such commencement, stand vacated; and, where, in pursuance of such attachment, any movable property of the bonded

labourer was seized and removed from his custody and kept in the custody of any court or other authority pending sale thereof, such movable property shall be restored, as soon as may be practicable after such commencement, to the possession of the bonded labourer.

(5) Where, before the commencement of this Act, possession of any property belonging to a bonded labourer or a member of his family or other dependent was forcibly taken over by any creditor for the recovery of any bonded debt, such property shall be restored, as soon as may be practicable after such commencement, to the possession of the person from whom it was seized.

(6) If restoration of the possession of any property referred to in sub-section (4) or sub-section (5) is not made within thirty days from the commencement of this Act, the aggrieved person may, within such time as may be prescribed, apply to the prescribed authority for the restoration of the possession of such property and the prescribed authority may, after giving the creditor a reasonable opportunity of being heard, direct the creditor to restore to the applicant the possession of the concerned property within such time as may be specified in the order.

(7) An order made by any prescribed authority, under sub-section (6), shall be deemed to be an order made by a civil court and may be executed by the court of the lowest pecuniary jurisdiction within the local of whose jurisdiction the creditor voluntarily resides or carries on business or personally works for gain.

(8) For the avoidance of doubts, it is hereby declared, that where any attached property was sold before the commencement of this Act, in execution of a decree or order for the recovery of a bonded debt, such sale shall not be affected by any provision of this Act. Provided that the bonded labourer, or an agent authorised by him in this behalf, may, at any time within five years from such commencement, apply to have the sale set aside on his

depositing in court, for payment to the decree-holder, the amount specified in the proclamation of sale, for the recovery of which the sale was ordered, less any amount, as well as mesne profits, which may, since the date of such proclamation of sale, have been received by the decree-holder.

(9) Where any suit or proceeding, for the enforcement of any obligation under the bonded labour system, including a suit or proceeding for the recovery of any advance made to a bonded labourer, is pending at the commencement of this Act, such suit or other proceeding shall, on such commencement stand dismissed.

(10) On the commencement of this Act, every bonded labourer who has been detained in civil prison, whether before or after judgment, shall be released from detention forthwith.

7. Property of Bonded Labourer to be Freed from Mortgage, etc.

(1) All property vested in a bonded labourer which was immediately before the commencement of this Act under any mortgage, charge, lien or other encumbrances in connection with any bonded debt shall, in so far as it is relatable to the bonded debt, stand freed and discharged from such mortgage, charge, lien or other encumbrances, and where any such property was, immediately before the commencement of this Act, in the possession of the mortgage or the holder of the charge, lien or encumbrance, such property shall (except where it was subject to any other charges), on such commencement, be restored to the possession of the bonded labourer.

(2) If any delay is made in restoring any property, referred to in sub-section (1), to the possession of the bonded labourer, such labourer shall be entitled, on and from the date of such commencement, to recover from the mortgage or holder of the lien, charge or encumbrance, such mesne profits as may be determined by the civil court of the lowest

pecuniary jurisdiction within the local limits of whose jurisdiction such property is situated.

8. Freed Bonded Labourer not to be Evicted from Homestead, etc.

(1) No person who has been freed and discharged under this Act from any obligation to render any bonded labour, shall be evicted from any homestead or other residential premises which he was occupying immediately before the commencement of this Act as part of the consideration for the bonded labour.

(2) If, after the commencement of this Act, any such person is evicted by the creditor from any homestead or other residential premises, referred to in sub-section (1), the Executive Magistrate in charge of the Sub-Division within which such homestead or residential premises is situated shall, as practicable, restore the bonded labourer to the possession of such homestead or other residential premises.

9. Creditor not to Accept Payment against Extinguished Debt

(1) No creditor shall accept any payment against any bonded debt which has been extinguished or deemed to have been extinguished or fully satisfied by virtue of the provisions of this Act.

(2) Whoever contravenes the provisions of sub-section (1), shall be punishable with imprisonment for a term which may extend to three years and also with fine.

(3) The court, convicting any person under sub-section (2) may, in addition to the penalties which may be imposed under that sub-section, direct the person to deposit, in court, the amount accepted in contravention of the provisions of sub-section (1), within such period as may be specified in the order for being refunded to the bonded labourer.

10. Authorities who may be Specified for Implementing the Provisions of this Act

The State Government may confer such powers and impose such duties on a District Magistrate as may be necessary to ensure that the provisions of this Act are properly carried out and the District Magistrate may specify the officer, subordinate to him, who shall exercise all or any of the powers, and perform all or any of the duties, so conferred or imposed and the local limits within which such powers or duties shall be carried out by the officer so specified.

11. Duty of District Magistrate and other Officers to Ensure Credit

The District Magistrate authorised by the State Government under Section 10 and the officer specified by the District Magistrate under that section shall, as far as practicable, try to promote the welfare of the freed bonded labourer by securing and protecting the economic interests of such bonded labourer so that he may not have any occasion or reason to contract any further bonded debt.

12. Duty of District Magistrate and Officers Authorised by him

It shall be the duty of every District Magistrate and every officer specified by him under Section 10 to inquire whether, after the commencement of this Act, any bonded labour system or any other form of forced labour is being enforced by, or on behalf of, any person resident within the local limits of his jurisdiction and if, as a result of such inquiry, any person is found to be enforcing the bonded labour system or any other system of forced labour, he shall forthwith take such action as may be necessary to eradicate of such forced labour.

Comment: whenever it is shown that a labourer is made to provide forced labour, the Court would raise a presumption that he is required to do so in consideration of an advance or other economic consideration received by him and he is therefore a bonded labourer. This presumption may be rebutted by the employer and also by the

State Government if it so chooses but unless and until satisfactory material is produced for rebutting this presumption, the Court must proceed on the basis that the labourer is a bonded labourer entitled to the benefit of thc provisions of the Act. *Bandhua Mukti Morcha,* v. *Union of India and others,* AIR 1984 S C 802.

13. Vigilance Committee

(1) Every State Government shall, by notification in the Official Gazette, constitute such number of Vigilance Committees in each district and each Sub-Division as it may think fit.

(2) Each Vigilance Committee, constituted for a district, shall consist of the following members, namely—

(a) the District Magistrate, or a person nominated by him, who shall be the Chairman;

(b) three persons belonging to the Scheduled Castes or Scheduled Tribes and residing in the District, to be nominated by the District Magistrate;

(c) two social workers, resident in the district, to be nominated by the District Magistrate;

(d) not more than three persons to represent the official or non-official agencies in the district connected with rural development, to be nominated by the State Government;

(e) one person to represent the financial and credit institutions in the district, to be nominated by the District Magistrate.

(3) Each Vigilance Committee, constituted for a Sub-Division, shall consist of the following members, namely—

(a) the Sub-Divisional Magistrate, or a person nominated by him, who shall be the Chairman;

(b) three persons belonging to the Scheduled Castes or Scheduled Tribes and residing in the Sub-Division, to be nominated by the Sub-Divisional Magistrate;

(c) two social workers, resident in the Sub-Division to be nominated by the Sub-Divisional Magistrate;
(d) not more than three persons to represent the official or non-official agencies in the Sub-Division connected with rural development to be nominated by the District Magistrate;
(e) one person to represent the financial and credit institutions in the Sub-Division, to be nominated by the Sub-Divisional Magistrate;
(f) one officer specified under Section 10 and functioning in the Sub-Division.

(4) Each Vigilance Committee shall regulate its own procedure and secretarial assistance, as may be necessary, shall be provided by—

(a) the District Magistrate, in the case of a Vigilance Committee constituted for the district;
(b) the Sub-Divisional Magistrate, in the case of a Vigilance Committee constituted for the Sub-Division.

(5) No proceeding of a Vigilance Committee shall be invalid by reason of any defect in the constitution, or in the proceedings, of the Vigilance Committee.

14. Repealed

15. Burden of Proof

Whenever any debt is claimed by a bonded labourer, or a Vigilance Committee, to be a bonded debt, the burden of proof that such debt is not a bonded debt shall lie on the creditor.

16. Punishment for Enforcement of Bonded Labour

Whoever, after the commencement of this Act, compels any person to render any bonded labour shall be punishable with imprisonment for a term which may extend to three years and also with fine which may extend to two thousand rupees.

17. Punishment for Advancement of Bonded Debt

Whoever advances, after the commencement of this Act, any bonded debt shall be punishable with imprisonment for a term which may extend to three years and also with fine which may extend to two thousand rupees.

18. Punishment for Extracting Bonded Labour under the Bonded Labour System

Whoever enforces, after the commencement of this Act, any custom, tradition, contract, agreement or other instrument, by virtue of which any person or any member of the family of such person or any dependent of such person is required to render any service under the bonded labour system, shall be punishable with imprisonment for a term which may extend to three years and also with fine which may extend to two thousand rupees; and, out of the fine, if recovered, payment shall be made to the bonded labourer at the rate of rupees five for each day for which the bonded labour was extracted from him.

19. Punishment for Omission or Failure to Restore Possession of Property to Bonded Labourers

Whoever, being required by this Act to restore any property to the possession of any bonded labourer, omits or fails to do so, within a period of thirty days from the commencement of this Act, shall be punishable with imprisonment for a term which may extend to one year, or with fine which may extend to one thousand rupees, or with both; and, out of the fine, if recovered, payment shall be made to the bonded labourer at the rate of rupees five for each day during which possession of the property was not restored to him.

20. Abetment to be an Offence

Whoever abets any offence punishable under this Act shall, whether or not the offence abetted is committed, be punishable with the same punishment as is provided for the offence which has been abetted.

Explanation : For the purpose of this Act, "abetment" has the meaning assigned to it in the Indian Penal Code (45 of 1860).

21. Offences to be Tried by Executive Magistrates

(1) The State Government may confer, on an Executive Magistrate, the powers of a Judicial Magistrate of the first class or of the second class for the trial of offences under this Act; and, on such conferment of powers, the Executive Magistrate, on whom the powers are so conferred, shall be deemed, for the purposes of the Code of Criminal Procedure, 1973 (2 of 1974), to be a Judicial Magistrate of the first class, or of the second class, as the case may be.

(2) An offence under this Act may be tried summarily by a Magistrate.

22. Cognizance of Offences

Every offence under this Act shall be cognizable and bailable.

23. Offences by Companies

(1) Where any offence under this Act has been committed by a company, every person who, at the time the offence was committed, was in charge of, and was responsible to, the company for the conduct of the business of the company, as well as the company, shall be deemed to be guilty of the offence and shall be liable to be proceeded against and punished accordingly.

(2) Notwithstanding anything contained in sub-section (1),

where any offence under this Act has been committed by a company and it is proved that the offence has been committed with the consent or connivance of, or is attributable to, any neglect on the part of, any director, manager, secretary or other officer of the company, such director, manager, secretary or other officer shall be deemed to be guilty of that offence and shall be liable to be proceeded against and punished accordingly.

Explanation : For the purposes of this section—

(a) "company" means any body corporate and includes a firm or other association of individual; and

(b) "director", in relation to a firm, means a partner in the firm.

24. Protection of Action Taken in Good Faith

No suit, prosecution or other legal proceeding shall lie against any officer of the State Government or any member of the Vigilance Committee for anything which is in good faith done or intended to be done under this Act.

25. Jurisdiction of Civil Courts Barred

No civil court shall have jurisdiction in respect of any matter to which any provision of this Act applies and no injunction shall be granted by any civil court in respect of anything which is done or intended to be done by or under this Act.

26. Power to make Rules

(1) The Central Government may, by notification in the Official Gazette, make rules for carrying out the provisions of this Act.

(2) In particular, and without prejudice to the foregoing power, such rules may provide for all or any of the following matters, namely—

(a) the authority to which application for the restoration of possession of property referred to in sub-section (4), or sub- section (5), of Section 6 is to be submitted of sub-section (6) of that section.
(b) the time within which application for restoration of possession of property is to be made, under sub-section (6) of Section 6, to the prescribed authority;
(c) steps to be taken by Vigilance Committee under clause (a) of sub-section (1) of Section 14, to ensure the implementation of the provisions of this Act or of any rule made there under;
(d) any other matter which is required to be, or may be, prescribed.

(3) Every rule made by the Central Government under this Act shall be laid, as soon as may be after it is made, before each House of Parliament while it is session, for a total period of thirty days which may be comprised in one session or in two or more successive sessions, and if, before the expiry of the session immediately following the session or successive sessions aforesaid, both Houses agree in making any modification in the rule of both Houses agree that the rule should not be made, the rule shall thereafter have effect only in such modified form or be of no effect, as the case may be; so, however, that any such modification or annulment shall be without prejudice to the validity of anything previously done under that rule.

27. Repeal and Saving

(1) The Bonded Labour System (Abolition) Ordinance, 1975 (17 of 1975)is hereby repealed.
(2) Notwithstanding such repeal, anything done or any action taken under the Ordinance (including any notification published, direction or nomination made, power conferred, duty imposed or officer specified) shall be deemed to have been done or taken under the corresponding provisions of this Act.

Annexure-3

THE AGRICULTURISTS' LOANS ACT, 1884

ACT NO.12 OF 1884 (AS ON 1955)

[It has been amended in –
C.P. and Berar by C.P. & Berar Acts 34 of 1947 and 54 of 1949;
Coorg by Coorg Act 3 of 1936;
Madras by Madras Act 16 of 1935;
Orissa by Orissa Act 6 of 1937; and
U.P. by U.P. Acts 12 of 1922, 12 of 1934 and 12 of 1948.]
An Act to amend and provide for the extension of the Northern India
Takkavi Act, 1879 [24th July, 1884]
WHEREAS it is expedient to amend the Northern India Takkavi Act, 1879, and provide for its extension to [Subs.by the A.O.1948, for "any part of British India"] [other (Subs. by the A.O.1950, for provinces of India)] [Part A States or Part C States]; It is hereby enacted as follows: – (Preamble.)

1. Short title

(1) This Act may be called the Agriculturists' Loans Act, 1884; and

(2) It shall come into force on the first day of August, 1884. (Commencement.)

2. Local extent

(1) This Section and Section 3 extend to the whole of India except Part B States.

(2) The rest of this Act extends in the first instance only to (Subs. by the A.O.1948, for original words.) [Bombay, Uttar Pradesh, Punjab, the Central Provinces, Assam, Delhi and Ajmer-Merwara.]

(3) But any State Government may, from time to time, by notification in the Official Gazette, extend the rest of this Act to the whole or any part of the territories under its administration.

3. [Repeal of Act X of 1879, and Sections 4 and 5 of Act XV of 1880.] Rep. by the Repealing Act, 1938 (1 of 1938), Sec. 2 and Sch.

4. Power for State Government to make rules

(1) State Government (Ins. by the Act 4 of 1914, Sec.2 and Sch. Pt.I.) [or, in a State for which there is a Board of Revenue or Financial Commissioner, such Board or Financial Commissioner, Subject to the control of the State Government] may, from time to time, (The words "subject to the control of the G.G.in C." rep. *ibid.*) make rules as to loans to be made to owners and occupiers of arable land, for the relief of distress, the purchase of seed or cattle, or any other purpose not specified in the Land Improvement Loans Act, 1883, but connected with agricultural objects.

(2) All such rules shall be published in the Official Gazette.

5. Recovery of loans

Every loan made in accordance with such rules, all interest (if any) chargeable thereon, and costs (if any) incurred in making or recovering the same, shall, when they become due, be recoverable from the person to whom the loan was made, or from any person who has become surety for the repayment thereof, as if they were arrears of land-revenue or costs incurred in recovering the same due by the person to whom the loan was made or by his surety.

6. Liability of joint Borrowers as among themselves

When a loan is made under this Act, to the members of a village community or to any other persons such terms that all of them arc jointly and severally bound to the Government for the payment of the whole amount payable in respect thereof, and a statement showing the portion of that amount which as among themselves each is bound to contribute is entered upon the order granting the loan and is signed, marked, or sealed by each of them or his agent duly authorised in this behalf and by the officer making the order, that statement shall be conclusive evidence of the portion of that amount which as among themselves each of those persons is bound to contribute.

Annexure-4

MINIMUM WAGES ACT, 1948

[ACT NO. 11 OF YEAR 1948, DATED 15TH MARCH, 1948]

(RELEVANT PORTIONS ONLY)

An Act to provide for fixing minimum rates of wages in certain employments, whereas it is expedient to provide for fixing minimum rates of wages in certain employments;

It is hereby enacted as follows:—

1. Short title and extent

(1) This Act may be called the Minimum Wages Act, 1948.
(2) It extends to the whole of India.

2. Interpretation

In this Act, unless there is anything repugnant in the subject or context,

[(a) "adolescent" means a person who has completed his fourteenth years of age but has not completed his eighteenth year;

(aa) "adult" means a person who has completed his eighteenth years of age;]

(b) "appropriate government" means—

(i) in relation to any scheduled employment carried on by or under the authority of the [Central Government or a railway administration], or in relation to a mine, oilfield or major port, or any corporation established by [a Central Act], the Central Government, and

(ii) in relation to any other scheduled employment, the State Government;

(bb) "child" means a person who has not completed his fourteenth year of age;

(c) "competent authority" means the authority appointed by the appropriate government by notification in its Official Gazette to ascertain from time to time the cost of living index number applicable to the employees employed in the scheduled employments specified in such notification;

(d) "cost of living index number" in relation to employees in any scheduled employment in respect of which minimum rates of wages have been fixed, means the index number ascertained and declared by the competent authority by notification in the Official Gazette to be the cost of living index number applicable to employees in such employment;

(e) "employer" means any person who employs, whether directly or through another person, or whether on behalf of himself or any other person, one or more employees in any scheduled employment in respect of which minimum rates of wages have been fixed under this Act, and includes, except in sub-section (3) of Section 26,-

(i) in a factory where there is carried on any scheduled employment in respect of which minimum rates of wages have been fixed under this Act, any person named under [clause (f) of sub-section (1) of Section 7 of the Factories Act, 1948 (63 of 1948)], as manager of the factory;

(ii) in any scheduled employment under the control of any government in India in respect of which minimum rates of wages have been fixed under this Act, the person or authority appointed by such government, for the supervision and control of employees or where no person or authority is so appointed the head of the department;

(iii) in any scheduled employment under any local authority in respect of which minimum rates of wages have been fixed under this Act, the person appointed by such authority for the supervision and control of employees or where no person is so appointed, the chief executive officer of the local authority;

(iv) in any other case where there is carried on any scheduled employment in respect of which minimum rates of wages have been fixed under this Act, any person responsible to the owner for the supervision and control of the employees or for the payment of wages;

(f) "prescribed" means prescribed by rules made under this Act;

(g) "scheduled employment" means an employment specified in the Schedule, or any process or branch of work forming part of such employment;

(h) "wages" means all remuneration, capable of being expressed in terms of money, which would, if the terms of the contract of employment, express or implied, were fulfilled, be payable to a person employed in respect of his employment or of work done in such employment [and includes house rent allowance], but does not include—

(i) the value of— (a) any house, accommodation, supply of light, water, medical attendance, or

(b) any other amenity or any service excluded by general or special order of the appropriate government;

(ii) any contribution paid by the employer to any pension fund or provident fund or under any scheme of social insurance;

(iii) any travelling allowance or the value of any travelling concession;

(iv) any sum paid to the person employed to defray special expenses entailed on him by the nature of his employment; or

(v) any gratuity payable on discharge; (i) "employee" means any person who is employed for hire or reward to do any work, skilled or unskilled, manual or clerical, in a scheduled employment in respect of which minimum rates of wages have been fixed; and includes an out-worker to whom any articles or materials are given out by another person to be made up, cleaned, washed, altered, ornamented, finished, repaired, adapted or otherwise processed for sale for the purposes of the trade or business of that other person where the process is to be carried out either in the home of the out-worker or in some other premises not being premises under the control and management of that other person; and also includes an employee declared to be an employee by the appropriate government; but does not include any member of the Armed Forces of the (Union).

3. Fixing of minimum rates of wages

[(1) The appropriate government shall, in the manner hereinafter provided,—[(a) fix the minimum rates of wages payable to employees employed in an employment specified in Part I or Part II of the Schedule and in an employment added to either Part by notification under Section 27:

PROVIDED that the appropriate Government may, in respect of employees employed in an employment specified in Part II of the Schedule, instead of fixing minimum rates of wages under this clause for the whole State, fix such rates for a part of the State or for any specified class or classes of such employment in the whole State or part thereof;]

(b) review at such intervals as it may think fit, such intervals not exceeding five years, the minimum rates of wages so fixed and revise the minimum rates, if necessary:

[PROVIDED that where for any reason the appropriate government has not reviewed the minimum rates of wages fixed by it in respect of any scheduled employment within any interval of five years, nothing contained in this clause shall be deemed to prevent it from reviewing the minimum rates after the expiry of the said period of five years and revising them, if necessary, and until they are so revised the minimum rates in force immediately before the expiry of the said period of five years shall continue in force.]

(1A) Notwithstanding anything contained in sub-section (1), the appropriate government may refrain from fixing minimum rates of wages in respect of any scheduled employment in which there are in the whole State less than one thousand employees engaged in such employment, but if at any time, the appropriate government comes to a finding after such inquiry as it may make or cause to be made in this behalf that the number of employees in any scheduled employment in respect of which it has refrained from fixing minimum rates of wages has risen to one thousand or more, it shall fix minimum rates of wages payable to employees in such employment [as soon as may be after such finding.]

(2) The appropriate government may fix—

(a) a minimum rate of wages for time work (hereinafter referred to as "a minimum time rate");

(b) a minimum rate of wages for piece work (hereinafter referred to as "a minimum piece rate");

(c) a minimum rate of remuneration to apply in the case of employees employed on piece work for the purpose of securing to such employees a minimum rate of wages on a time work basis (hereinafter referred to as "a guaranteed time rate");

(d) a minimum rate (whether a time rate or a piece rate) to apply in substitution for the minimum rate which would otherwise be applicable, in respect of overtime work done by employees (hereinafter referred to as "overtime rate").

[(2A) Where in respect of an industrial dispute relating to the rates of wages payable to any of the employees employed in a scheduled employment, any proceeding is pending before a Tribunal or National Tribunal under the Industrial Disputes Act, 1947 (14 of 1947) or before any like authority under any other law for the time being in force, or an award made by any Tribunal, National Tribunal or such authority is in operation, and a notification fixing or revising the minimum rates of wages in respect of the scheduled employment is issued during the pendency of such proceeding or the operation of the award, then, notwithstanding anything contained in this Act, the minimum rates of wages so fixed or so revised shall not apply to those employees during the period in which the proceeding is pending and the award made therein is in operation or, as the case may be, where the notification is issued during the period of operation of an award, during that period; and where such proceeding or award relates to the rates of wages payable to all the employees in the scheduled employment, no minimum rates of wages shall be fixed or revised in respect of that employment during the said period.]

(3) In fixing or revising minimum rates of wages under this Section,—

(a) different minimum rates of wages may be fixed for—

(i) different scheduled employments;

(ii) different classes of work in the same scheduled employment;

(iii) adults, adolescents, children and apprentices;

(iv) different localities;

[(b) minimum rates of wages may be fixed by any one or more of the following wage periods, namely:—

(i) by the hour,

(ii) by the day,

(iii) by the month, or

(iv) by such other larger wage-period as may be prescribed;

and where such rates are fixed by the day or by the month, the manner of calculating wages for a month or for a day, as the case may be, may be indicated:]

PROVIDED that where any wage-periods have been fixed under Section 4 of the Payment of Wages Act, 1936 (4 of 1936), minimum wages shall be fixed in accordance therewith.

4. Minimum rates of wages

(1) Any minimum rates of wages fixed or revised by the appropriate government in respect of scheduled employments under Section 3 may consist of—

(i) a basic rate of wages and a special allowance at a rate to be adjusted, at such intervals and in such manner as the appropriate government may direct, to accord as nearly as practicable with the variation in the cost of living index number applicable to such workers (hereinafter referred to as the "cost of living allowance"); or

(ii) a basic rate of wages with or without the cost of living allowance, and the cash value of the concessions in respect of supplies of essential commodities at concessional rates, where so authorised; or

(iii) an all-inclusive rate allowing for the basic rate, the cost of living allowance and the cash value of the concessions, if any.

(2) The cost of living allowance and the cash value of the concessions in respect of supplies of essential commodities at concessional rate shall be computed by the competent authority at such intervals and in accordance with such directions as may be specified or given by the appropriate government.

5. Procedure for fixing and revising minimum wages

(1) In fixing minimum rates of wages in respect of any scheduled employment for the first time under this Act or

in revising minimum rates of wages so fixed, the appropriate government shall either—

(a) appoint as many committees and sub-committees as it considers necessary to hold enquiries and advise it in respect of such fixation or revision, as the case may be, or

(b) by notification in the Official Gazette, publish its proposals for the information of persons likely to be affected thereby and specify a date, not less than two months from the date of the notification, on which the proposals will be taken into consideration.

(2) After considering the advice of the committee or committees appointed under clause (a) of sub-section (1), or as the case may be, all representations received by it before the date specified in the notification under clause (b) of that sub-section, the appropriate government shall, by notification in the Official Gazette fix, or, as the case may be, revise the minimum rates of wages in respect of each scheduled employment, and unless such notification otherwise provides, it shall come into force on the expiry of three months from the date of its issue:

PROVIDED that where the appropriate government proposes to revise the minimum rate of wages by the mode specified in clause (b) of sub-section (1), the appropriate government shall consult the Advisory Board also.]

6. Advisory committees and sub-committees

[Repealed by the Minimum Wages (Amendment) Act, 1957 (30 of 1957).]

7. Advisory Board

For the purpose of co-ordinating work of [committees and sub-committees appointed under Section 5] and advising the appropriate government generally in the matter of fixing and revising minimum rate of wages, the appropriate government shall appoint an Advisory Board.

8. Central Advisory Board

(1) For the purpose of advising the Central and State Governments in the matters of the fixation and revision of minimum rates of wages and other matters under this Act and for co-ordinating the work of the Advisory Boards, the Central Government shall appoint a Central Advisory Board.

(2) The Central Advisory Board shall consist of persons to be nominated by the Central Government representing employers and employees in the scheduled employments, who shall be equal in number, and independent persons not exceeding one-third of its total number of members; one of such independent persons shall be appointed the Chairman of the Board by the Central Government.

9. Composition of committees, etc.

Each of the committees, sub-committees and the Advisory Board shall consist of persons to be nominated by the appropriate government representing employers and employees in the scheduled employments, who shall be equal in number, and independent persons not exceeding one-third of its total number of members; one of such independent persons shall be appointed the Chairman by the appropriate government.

10. Correction of errors

(1) The appropriate government may, at any time, by notification in the Official Gazette, correct clerical or arithmetical mistakes in any order fixing or revising minimum rates of wages under this Act, or errors arising therein from any accidental slip or omission.

(2) Every such notification shall, as soon as may be after it is issued, be placed before the Advisory Board for information.

11. Wages in kind

(1) Minimum wages payable under this Act shall be paid in cash.

(2) Where it has been the custom to pay wages wholly or partly in kind, the appropriate government being of the opinion that it is necessary in the circumstances of the case may, by notification in the Official Gazette, authorise the payment of minimum wages either wholly or partly in kind.

(3) If appropriate government is of the opinion that provision should be made for the supply of essential commodities at concessional rates, the appropriate government may, by notification in the Official Gazette, authorise the provision of such supplies at concessional rates.

(4) The cash value of wages in kind and of concessions in respect of supplies of essential commodities at concessional rates authorised under sub-sections (2) and (3) shall be estimated in the prescribed manner.

12. Payment of minimum rates of wages

(1) Where in respect of any scheduled employment a notification under Section 5 is in force, the employer shall pay to every employee engaged in a scheduled employment under him wages at a rate not less than the minimum rate of wages fixed by such notification for that class of employees in that employment without any deductions except as may be authorised within such time and subject to such conditions as may be prescribed.

(2) Nothing contained in this section shall affect the provisions of the Payment of Wages Act, 1936 (4 of 1936).

13. Fixing hours for a normal working day, etc.

(1) In regard to any scheduled employment minimum rates of wages in respect of which have been fixed under this Act, the appropriate government may—

(a) fix the number of hours of work which shall constitute a normal working day, inclusive of one or more specified intervals;

(b) provide for a day of rest in every period of seven days

which shall be allowed to all employees or to any specified class of employees and for the payment of remuneration in respect of such days of rest;

(c) provide for payment for work on a day of rest at a rate not less than the overtime rate.

[(2) The provisions of sub-Section (1) shall, in relation to the following classes of employees, apply only to such extent and subject to such conditions as may be prescribed:—

(a) employees engaged on urgent work, or in any emergency which could not have been foreseen or prevented;

(b) employees engaged in work in the nature of preparatory or complementary work which must necessarily be carried on outside the limits laid down for the general working in the employment concerned;

(c) employees whose employment is essentially intermittent;

(d) employees engaged in any work which for technical reasons has to be completed before the duty is over;

(e) employees engaged in a work which could not be carried on except at times dependent on the irregular action of natural forces.

(3) For the purposes of clause (c) of sub-section (2), employment of an employee is essentially intermittent when it is declared to be so by the appropriate government on the ground that the daily hours of duty of the employee, or if there be no daily hours of duty as such for the employee, the hours of duty, normally include periods of inaction during which the employee may be on duty but is not called upon to display either physical activity or sustained attention.]

Annexure-5

WORKMEN'S COMPENSATION ACT, 1923

(RELEVANT PORTIONS ONLY)

CHAPTER I: PRELIMINARY

1. Short Title, extend and commencement

(1) This Act may be called the Workmen's Compensation Act, 1923.
(2) It extends to the whole of India.
(3) It shall come into force on the first day of July, 1924.

2. Definitions in this Act unless there is anything repugnant in the subject or context

[Clause (a) omitted w.e.f. 1-6-1959.]
(b) "Commissioner" means a Commissioner for Workmen's Compensation appointed under Section 20;
(c) "compensation" means compensation as provided for by this Act;
(d) "dependent" means any of the following relatives of a deceased workman namely :—
 (i) a widow a minor legitimate or adopted son an unmarried legitimate or adopted daughter or a widowed mother; and
 (ii) if wholly dependant on the earnings of the workman at the time of his death a son or a daughter who has attained the age of 18 years and who is infirm;

(iii) if wholly or in part dependant on the earnings of the workman at the time of his death—

(a) a widower

(b) a parent other than a widowed mother

(c) a minor illegitimate son an unmarried illegitimate daughter or a daughter legitimate or illegitimate or adopted if married and a minor or if widowed and minor

(d) a minor brother or an unmarried sister or a widowed sister if a minor

(e) a widowed daughter-in-law

(f) a minor child of a pre-deceased son

(g) a minor child of a pre-deceased daughter where no parent of the child is alive, or

(h) a paternal grandparent if no parent of the workman is alive;

Explanation : For the purpose of sub-clause (ii) and items (f) and (g) of sub-clause (iii) references to a son daughter or child include an adopted son daughter or child respectively.

(e) "employer" includes any body of persons whether incorporated or not and any managing agent of an employer and the legal representative of a deceased employer and when the services of a workman are temporarily lent or let on hire to another person by the person with whom the workman has entered into a contract of service or apprenticeship means such other person while the workman is working for him;

(f) "managing agent" means any person appointed or acting as the representative of another person for the purpose of carrying on such other person's trade or business but does not include an individual manager subordinate to an employer;

(ff) "minor" means a person who has not attained the age of 18 years;

(g) "partial disablement" means where the disablement is of a temporary nature such disablement as reduces the earning capacity of a workman in any employment in which he was engaged at the time of the accident resulting in the disablement and where the disablement is of a permanent nature such disablement as reduces his earning capacity in every employment which he was capable of undertaking at that time :

Provided that every injury specified in Part II of Schedule shall be deemed to result in permanent partial disablement;

(h) "prescribed" means prescribed by rules made under this Act;

(i) "qualified medical practitioner" means any person registered under any Central Act or an Act of the Legislature of a State providing for the maintenance of a register of medical practitioners or in any area where no such last-mentioned Act is in force any person declared by the State Government by notification in the Official Gazette to be a qualified medical practitioner for the purpose of this Act; [Clause (j) omitted by Act 15 of 1933]

(k) "seaman" means any person forming part of the crew of any ship but does not include the master of the ship;

(l) "total disablement" means such disablement whether of a temporary or permanent nature as incapacitates a workman for all work which he was capable of performing at the time of the accident resulting in such disablement :
Provided that permanent total disablement shall be deemed to result from every injury specified in Part I of Schedule I or from any combination of injuries specified in Part II thereof where the aggregate percentage of the loss of earning capacity as specified in the said Part II against those injuries amount to one hundred per cent or more;

(m) "wages" includes any privilege or benefit which is capable of being estimated in money other than a travelling allowance or the value of any travelling concession or a contribution paid by the employer of a workman towards any pension or provident fund or a sum paid to a workman to cover any special expenses entailed on him by the nature of his employment;

(n) "workman" means any person (other than a person whose employment is of a casual nature and who is employed otherwise than for the purposes of the employer's trade or business) who is—

(i) a railway servant as defined in Section 3 of the Indian Railways Act, 1890 (9 of 1890) not permanently employed in any administrative district or sub-divisional office of a railway and not employed in any such capacity as is specified in Schedule II or (ia)(a) a master seaman or other member of the crew of a ship, (b) a captain or other member of the crew of an aircraft, (c) a person recruited as driver helper mechanic cleaner or in any other capacity in connection with a motor vehicle, (d) a person recruited for work abroad by a company and who is employed outside India in any such capacity as is specified in Schedule II and the ship aircraft or motor vehicle or company as the case may be is registered in India or;

(ii) employed in any such capacity as is specified in Schedule II whether the contract of employment was made before or after the passing of this Act and whether the contract is expressed or implied oral or in writing; but does not include any person working in the capacity of a member of the Armed Forces of the Union; and any reference to a workman who has been injured shall where the workman is dead includes a reference to his dependants or any of them.

(2) The exercise and performance of the powers and duties of a local authority or of any department acting on behalf of the Government shall for the purposes of this Act unless a

contrary intention appears be deemed to be the trade or business of such authority or department.

(3) The Central Government or the State Government after giving by notification in the Official Gazette not less than three months' notice of its intention so to do may by a like notification add to Schedule II any class of persons employed in any occupation which it is satisfied is a hazardous occupation and the provisions of this Act shall thereupon apply in case of notification by the Central Government within the territories to which the Act extends or in the case of a notification by a State Government within the State to such classes of persons :

Provided that in making addition the Central Government or the State Government as the case may be may direct that the provisions of this Act shall apply to such classes of persons in respect of specified injuries only.

CHAPTER II : WORKMEN'S COMPENSATION

3. Employer's liability for compensation

(1) If personal injury is caused to a workman by accident arising out of and in the course of his employment his employer shall be liable to pay compensation in accordance with the provisions of this Chapter:

Provided that the employer shall not be so liable —

(a) in respect of any injury which does not result in the total or partial disablement of the workman for a period exceeding three days;

(b) in respect of any injury not resulting in death or permanent total disablement caused by an accident which is directly attributable to —

the workman having been at the time thereof under the influence of drink or drugs or the wilful disobedience of the workman to an order expressly given or to a rule expressly framed for the purpose of securing the safety of workmen or the wilful removal or disregard by the workman of any safety guard or other device he knew to have been provided for the purpose of securing the safety of workman.

(2) If a workman employed in any employment specified in Part A of Schedule III contracts any disease specified therein as an occupational disease peculiar to that employment or if a workman whilst in the service of an employer in whose service he has been employed for a continuous period of not less than six months (which period shall not include a period of service under any other employer in the same kind of employment) in any employment specified in Part B of Schedule III contracts any disease specified therein as an occupational disease peculiar to that employment or if a workman whilst in the service of one or more employers in any employment specified in Part C of Schedule III for such continuous period as the Central Government may specify in respect of each such employment contracts any disease specified therein as an occupational disease peculiar to that employment the contracting of the disease shall be deemed to be as injury by accident within the meaning of this section and unless the contrary is proved the accident shall be deemed to have arisen out of and in the course of the employment :

Provided that if it proved —

that a workman whilst in the service of one or more employers in any employment specified in Part C of Schedule III has contracted a disease specified therein as an occupational disease peculiar to that employment during a continuous period which is less than the period specified under this sub-Section for that employment; and that the disease has arisen out of and in the course of the employment the contracting of such disease shall be deemed to be an injury by accident within the meaning of this Section :

Provided further that if it is proved that a workman who having served under any employer in any employment specified in Part B of Schedule III or who having served under one or more employers in any employment specified in Part C of that Schedule for a continuous period specified under this sub-Section for that employment and he has after the cessation of such service contracted any disease specified in the said Part B or the said Part C as the case may be as an occupational disease peculiar to the employment and that such disease arose out of the employment the contracting of the disease shall be deemed to be injury by accident within the meaning of this Section.

(2A) If a workman employed in any employment specified in Part C of Schedule III contracts any occupational disease peculiar to that employment the contracting whereof is deemed to be an injury by accident within the meaning of this Section and such employment was under more than one employer all such employers shall be liable for the payment of the compensation in such proportion as the Commissioner may in the circumstances deem just.

(3) The Central Government or the State Government after giving by notification in the Official Gazette not less than three months' notice of its intention so to do may by a like notification add any description of employment to the employments specified in Schedule III and shall specify in the case of employments so added the diseases which shall be deemed for the purposes of this Section to be occupational diseases peculiar to those employments respectively and thereupon the provisions of sub-section (2) shall apply in the case of a notification by the Central Government within the territories to which this Act extends or in case of and notification by the State Government within the State as if such diseases had been declared by this Act to be occupational diseases peculiar to those employments.

Save as provided by sub-sections (2), (2A) and (3) no compensation shall be payable to a workman in respect of any disease unless the disease is directly attributable to a specific injury by accident arising out of and in the course of his employment. Nothing herein contained shall be deemed to confer any right to compensation on a workman in respect of any injury if he has instituted in a civil court a suit for damages in respect of the injury against the employer or any other person; and no suit for damages shall be maintainable by a workman in any court of law in respect of any injury —

(a) if he has instituted a claim to compensation in respect of the injury before a Commissioner; or

(b) if an agreement has been made between the workman and his employer providing for the payment of compensation in respect of the injury in accordance with the provisions of this Act.

4. Amount of compensation

(1) Subject to the provisions of this Act the amount of compensation shall be as follows namelys:—

where death results from the injury an amount equal to fifty per cent of the monthly wages of the deceased workman multiplied by the relevant factor; or an amount of fifty thousand rupees whichever is more; where permanent total disablement results from the injury an amount equal to sixty per cent of the monthly wages of the injured workman multiplied by the relevant factor; or an amount of sixty thousand rupees whichever is more. *Explanation I*: For the purpose of clause (a) and clause (b) relevant factor in relation to a workman means the factor specified in the second column of Schedule IV against the entry in the fits column of that Schedule specifying the number of years which are the same as the completed years of the age of the workman on his birthday immediately preceding the date on which the compensation fell due;

Explanation II: Where the monthly wages of a workman exceed two thousand rupees his monthly wages for the purposes of clause (a) and clause (b) shall be deemed to be two thousand rupees only;

(c) where permanent partial disablement results from the injury in the case of an injury specified in Part II of Schedule I such percentage of the compensation which would have been payable in the case of permanent total disablement as is specified therein as being the percentage of the loss of earning capacity caused by that injury; and in the case of an injury specified in Schedule I such percentage of the compensation payable in the case of permanent total disablement as is proportionate to the loss of earning capacity (as assessed by the qualified medical practitioner) permanently caused by the injury.

Explanation I : Where more injuries than one are caused by the same accident the amount of compensation payable under this head shall be aggregated but not so in any case as to exceed the amount which would have been payable if permanent total disablement had resulted from the injuries.

Explanation II : In assessing the loss of earning capacity for the purpose of sub-clause (ii) the qualified medical practitioner shall have due regard to the percentages of loss of earning capacity in relation to different injuries specified in Schedule I;

(d) where temporary disablement whether total or partial results from the injury a half monthly payment of the sum equivalent to twenty-five per cent of monthly wages of the workman to be paid in accordance with the provisions of sub-section (2).

(1A) Notwithstanding anything contained in sub-section (1) while fixing the amount of compensation payable to a workman in respect of an accident occurred outside India the Commissioner shall take into account the amount of compensation if any awarded to such workman in accordance with the law of the country in which the compensation if any awarded to such workman in accordance with the law of the country in which the accident occurred and shall reduce the amount fixed by the amount of compensation awarded to the workman in accordance with the law of that country.

(2) The half-monthly payment referred to in clause (d) of sub-Section (1) shall be payable on the sixteenth day - from the date of disablement where such disablement lasts for a period of twenty-eight days or more or after the expiry of a waiting period of three days from the date of disablement where such disablement lasts for a period of less than twenty-eight days; and thereafter half-monthly during the disablement or during a period of five years whichever period is shorter :

Provided that—

There shall be deducted from any lump sum or half monthly payments to which the workman is entitled the amount of any payment or allowance which the workman has received from the employer by way of compensation during the period of disablement prior to the receipt of such lump sum or of the first half monthly payment as the case may be; and no half monthly payment shall in any case exceed the amount if any by which half the amount of the monthly wages of the workman before the accident exceeds half the amount of such wages which he is earning after the accident.

Explanation: Any payment or allowance which the workman has received from the employer towards his medical treatment shall not be deemed to be a payment or allowance received by him by way of compensation within the meaning of clause (a) of the proviso.

On the ceasing of the disablement before the date on which any half monthly payment falls due there shall be payable in respect of that half monthly a sum proportionate to the duration of the disablement in that half month. If the injury of the workman results in his death the employer shall in addition to the compensation under sub-section (1) deposit with the Commissioner a sum of one thousand rupees for payment of the same of the eldest surviving dependant of the workman towards the expenditure of the funeral of such workman or where the workman did not have a dependant or was not living with his dependant at the time of his death to the person who actually incurred such expenditure.

4A. Compensation to be paid when due and penalty for default

(1) Compensation under Section 4 shall be paid as soon as it falls due. (2) In cases where the employer does not accept the liability for compensation to the extent claimed he shall be bound to make provisional payment based on the extent of liability which he accepts and such payment shall be deposited with the Commissioner or made to the workman as the case may be without prejudice to the right of the workman to make any further claim.

Direct that the employer shall in addition to the amount of the arrears pay simple interest thereon at the rate of twelve per cent annum or at such higher rate not exceeding the maximum of the lending rates of any scheduled bank as may be specified by the Central Government by notification in the Official Gazette on the amount due; and if in his opinion there is no jurisdiction for the delay direct that the employer shall in addition to the amount of the arrears and interest thereon pay a further sum not exceeding fifty per cent of such amount by way of penalty :

Provided that an order for the payment of penalty shall not be passed under clause (b) without giving a reasonable opportunity to the employer to show cause why it should not be passed.

Explanation: For the purposes of this sub-section "scheduled bank" means a bank for the time being included in the Second Schedule to the Reserve Bank of India Act 1934 (2 of 1934).

(3A) The interest payable under sub-section (3) shall be paid to the workman or his dependant as the case may be and the penalty shall be credited to the State Government.

5. Method of Calculating Wages

Method of calculating wages in this Act and for the purpose thereof the expression "monthly wages" means the amount of wages deemed to be payable for a months' service (whether the wages are payable by the month or by whatever other period or at piece rates) and calculated as follows namely: —

where the workman has during a continuous period of not less than twelve months immediately preceding the accident been in the service of the employer who is liable to pay compensation the monthly wages of the workman shall be one-twelfth of the total wages which have fallen due for payment to him by the employer in the last twelve months of that period; where the whole of the continuous period of service immediately preceding the accident during which the workman was in the service of the employer who is liable to pay the compensation was less than one month the monthly wages of the workman shall be the average monthly amount which during the twelve months immediately preceding the accident was being earned by a workman employed on the same work by the same employer or if there was no workman so employed by a workman employed on similar work in the same locality; in other cases including cases in which it is not possible for want of necessary information to calculate the monthly wages under clause (b) the monthly wages shall be thirty times the total wages earned in respect of the last continuous period of service immediately preceding the accident from the employer who is liable to pay compensation divided by the number of days comprising such period.

Explanation : A period of service shall for the purposes of this Section be deemed to be continuous which has not been interrupted by a period of absence from work exceeding fourteen days.

6. Review any half-monthly payment payable under this Act

Either under an agreement between the parties or under the order of a Commissioner may be reviewed by the Commissioner on the application either of the employer or of the workman accompanied by the certificate of a qualified medical practitioner that there has been a change in the condition of the workman or subject to rules made under this Act on application made without such certificate. (2) Any half-monthly payment may on review under this section subject to the provisions of this Act be continued increased/ decreased or ended or if the accident is found to have resulted in permanent disablement be converted to the lump sum to which the workman is entitled less any amount which he has already received by way of half-monthly payments.

7. Commutation of half-monthly payments

Any right to receive half-monthly payments may by agreement between the parties or if the parties cannot agree and the payments have been continued for not less than six months on the application of either party to the Commissioner be redeemed by the payment of a lump sum of such amount as may be agreed to by the parties or determined by the Commissioner as the case may be.

8. Distribution of compensation

(1) No payment of compensation in respect of a workman whose injury has resulted in death and no payment of a lump sum as compensation to a woman or a person under a legal disability shall be made otherwise than by deposit with the Commissioner and no such payment directly by an employer shall be deemed to be a payment of compensation:

Provided that in the case of a deceased workman an employer may make to any dependant advances on account of compensation of an amount equal to ·hree months' wages of such workman and so much of such amount as does not exceed the compensation payable to that dependant shall be deducted by the Commissioner from such compensation and repaid to the employer.

Any other sum amounting to not less than ten rupees which is payable as compensation may be deposited with the Commissioner on behalf of the person entitled thereto. The receipt of the Commissioner shall be a sufficient discharge in respect of any compensation deposited with him. On the deposit of any money under sub-section (1) as compensation in respect of a deceased workman the Commissioner shall if he thinks necessary cause notice to be published or to be served on each dependant in such manner as he thinks fit calling upon the dependants to appear before him on such dates as he may fix for determining the distribution of the compensation. If the Commissioner is satisfied after any inquiry which he may deem necessary that no dependant exists he shall repay the balance of the money to the employer by whom it was paid. The Commissioner shall on application by the employer furnish a statement showing in detail all disbursements made. Compensation deposited in respect of a deceased workman shall subject to any deduction made under sub-section (4) be apportioned among the dependants of the deceased workman or any of them in such proportion as the Commissioner thinks fit or may in the desecration of the Commissioner be allotted to any one dependant. Where any compensation deposited with the Commissioner is payable to any person the Commissioner shall if the person to whom the compensation is payable is not a woman or a person under a legal disability and may in other cases pay the money to the person entitled thereto.

Where any lump sum deposited with the Commissioner is payable to a woman or a person under a legal disability such sum may be invested applied or otherwise dealt with for the benefit of the woman or of such person during his disability in such manner as the Commissioner may direct; and where a half-monthly payment is payable to any person under a legal disability the Commissioner may of his own motion or on an application made to him in this behalf order that the payment be made during the disability to any dependant of the workman or to any other person whom the Commissioner thinks best fitted to provide for the welfare of the workman. Where on application made to him in this behalf or otherwise the Commissioner is satisfied that on account of neglect of children on the part of a parent or on account of the variation of the circumstances of any dependant of for any other sufficient cause an order of the Commissioner as to the distribution of any sum paid as compensation or as to the manner in which any sum payable to any such dependant is to be invested applied or otherwise dealt with ought to be varied the Commissioner may make such order for the variation of the former order as he thinks just in the circumstances of the case :

Provided that no such order prejudicial to any person shall be made unless such person has been given an opportunity of showing cause why the order should not be made or shall be made in and case in which it would involve the repayment by a dependant of any sum already paid to him. (2) Where the Commissioner varies any order under sub-section (8) by reason of the fact that payment of compensation to any person has been obtained by fraud impersonation or other improper means any amount so paid to or on behalf of such person may be recovered in the manner hereinafter provided in Section 31.

9. Compensation not to be assigned attached or charged

Save as provided by this Act no lump sum or half-monthly payment payable under this Act shall in any way be capable of being assigned or charged or be liable to attachment or pass to any person other than the workman by operation of law nor shall any claim be set off against the same.

10. Notice and claim

(1) No claim for compensation shall be entertained by a Commissioner unless notice of the accident has been given in the manner hereinafter provided as soon as practicable after the happening thereof and unless the claim is preferred before him within two years of the occurrence of the accident or in case of death within two years from the date of death:

Provided that where the accident is the contracting of a disease in respect of which the provisions of sub-section (2) of Section 3 are applicable the accident shall be deemed to have occurred on the first of the days during which the workman was continuously absent from work in consequence of the disablement caused by the disease:

Provided further that in case of partial disablement due to the contracting of any such disease and which does not force the workman to absent himself from work the period of two years shall be counted from the day the workman gives notice of the disablement to his employer:

Provided further that if a workman who having been employed in an employment for a continuous period specified under sub-section (2) of Section 3 in respect of that employment ceases to be so employed and develops symptoms of an occupational disease peculiar to that employment within two years of the cessation of employment the accident shall be deemed to have occurred on the day on which the symptoms were first detected:

Provided further that the want of or any defect or irregularity in a notice shall not be a bar to the entertainment of a claim —

(a) if the claim is preferred in respect of the death of a workman resulting from an accident which occurred on the premises of the employer or at any place where the workman at the time of the accident was working under the control of the employer or of any person employed by him and the workman died on such premises or at such place or on any premises belonging to the employer or died without having left the vicinity of the premises or place where the accident occurred; or

(b) if the employer or any one of several employers or any person responsible to the employer for the management of any branch of the trade or business in which the injured workman was employed had knowledge of the accident from any other source at or about the time when it occurred :

Provided further that the Commissioner may entertain and decide any claim to compensation in any case notwithstanding that the notice has not been given or the claim has not been preferred in due time as provided in this sub-section if he is satisfied that the failure so to give the notice or prefer the claim as the case may be was due to sufficient cause.

(2) Every such notice shall give the name and address of the person injured and shall state in ordinary language the cause of the injury and the date on which the accident happened and shall be served on the employer or upon any one of several employers or upon any person responsible to the employer for the management of any branch of the trade or business in which the injured workman was employed.

(3) The State Government may require that any prescribed class of employers shall maintain at these premises at which workmen are employed a notice book in the prescribed

form which shall be readily accessible at all reasonable times to any injuries workman employed on the premises and to any person acting bona fide on his behalf.

(4) A notice under this Section may be served by delivering it at or sending it by registered post addressed to the residence or any office or place of business of the person on whom it is to be served or where a notice book is maintained by entry in the notice-book.

10A. Power to require from employers statements regarding fatal accident

(1) Where a Commissioner receives information from any source that a workman has died as a result of an accident arising out of and in the course of his employment he may send by registered post a notice to the workman's employer requiring him to submit within thirty days of the service of the notice a statement in the prescribed form giving the circumstances attending the death of the workman and indicating whether in the opinion of the employer he is or is not liable to deposit compensation on account of the death.

(2) If the employer is of opinion that he is liable to deposit compensation he shall make the deposit within thirty days of the service of the notice.

(3) If the employer is of opinion that he is not liable to deposit compensation he shall in his statement indicate the grounds on which he disclaims liability.

(4) Where the employer has so disclaimed liability the Commissioner after such inquiry as he may think fit may inform any of the dependants of the deceased workman that it is open to the dependants to prefer a claim for compensation and may give them such other further information as he may think fit.

10B. Reports of fatal accidents and serious bodily injuries

(1) Where by any law for the time being in force notice is

required to be given to any authority by or on behalf of an employer of any accident occurring on his premises which results in death or serious bodily injury the person required to give the notice shall within seven days of the death or serious bodily injury send a report to the Commissioner giving the circumstances attending the death or serious bodily injury:

Provided that where the State Government has so prescribed the person required to give the notice may instead of sending such report to the Commissioner send it to the authority to whom he is required to give the notice.

Explanation: "Serious bodily injury" means an injury which involves or in all probability will involve the permanent loss of the use of or permanent injury to any limb or the permanent loss of or injury to the sight or hearing or the fracture of any limb or the enforced absence of the injured person from work for a period exceeding twenty days.

(2) The State Government may by notification in the Official Gazette extend the provisions of sub-section (1) to any class of premises other than those coming within the scope of that sub-section and may by such notification specify the person who shall send the report to the Commissioner.

(3) Nothing in this Section shall apply to factories to which the Employees' State Insurance Act, 1948 (34 of 1948) applies.

11. Medical examination

(1) Where a workman has given notice of an accident he shall if the employer before the expiry of three days from the time at which service of the notice has been effected offers to have him examined free of charge by a qualified medical practitioner submit himself for such examination and any workman who is in receipt of a half-monthly payment under this Act shall if so required submit himself for such

examination from time to time :

Provided that a workman shall not be required to submit himself for examination by a medical practitioner otherwise than in accordance with rules made under this Act or at more frequent intervals than may be prescribed.

(2) If a workman on being required to do so by employer under sub-section (1) or by the Commissioner at any time refuses to submit himself for examination by a qualified medical practitioner or in any way obstructs the same his right to compensation shall be suspended during the continuance of such refusal or obstruction unless in the case of refusal he was prevented by any sufficient cause from so submitting himself.

(3) If a workman before the expiry of the period within which he is liable under sub-section (1) to be required to submit himself for medical examination voluntarily leaves without having been so examined the vicinity of the place in which he was employed his right to compensation shall be suspended until he returns and offers himself for such examination.

Where a workman whose right to compensation has been suspended under sub-section (2) or sub-section (3) dies without having submitted himself for medical examination as required by either of those sub-sections the Commissioner may if he thinks fit direct the payment of compensation to the dependants of the deceased workman. Where under sub-section (2) or sub-section (3) a right to compensation is suspended no compensation shall be payable in respect of the period of suspension and if the period of suspension commences before the expiry of the waiting period referred to in clause (d) of sub-section (1) of Section 4 the waiting period shall be increased by the period during which the suspension continues. Where an injured workman has refused to be attended by a qualified medical practitioner whose services have been offered to him by the employer free of charge or having accepted such offer has deliberately disregarded the instructions of such medical practitioner then if it is proved that the workman has not thereafter been regularly attended by a qualified medical practitioner or having been so attended has deliberately failed to follow his instructions and that such refusal disregard or failure was unreasonable in the circumstances of the case and that the injury has been aggravated thereby the injury and resulting disablement shall be deemed to be of the same nature and duration as they might reasonably have been excepted to be if the workman had been regularly attended by a qualified medical practitioner whose instructions he had followed and compensation if any shall be payable accordingly.

12. Contracting

Where any person (hereinafter in this Section referred to as the principal) in the course of or for the purposes of his trade or business contract with any other person (hereinafter in this Section referred to as the contractor for the execution by or under the contractor of the whole or any part of any work which is ordinarily part of the trade or business of the principal the principal shall be liable to pay to any workman employed in the execution of the work any compensation which he would have been liable to pay if that workman had been immediately employed by him; and where compensation is claimed from the principal this Act shall apply as if references to the principal were substituted for references to the employer except that the amount of compensation shall be calculated with reference to the wages of the workman under the employer by whom he is immediately employed. Where the principal is liable to pay compensation under this Section he shall be entitled to be indemnified by the contractor or any other person from whom the workman could have recovered compensation and where a contractor who is himself a principal is liable to pay compensation or to indemnify a principal under this Section shall be entitled to be indemnified by any person standing to him in the relation of a contractor from whom the workman could have recovered compensation and all questions as to the right to and the amount of any such indemnity shall in default of agreement be settled by the Commissioner. Nothing in this Section shall be construed as preventing a workman from recovering compensation from the contractor instead of the principal. This Section shall not apply in any case where the accident occurred elsewhere that on in or about the premises on which the principal has undertaken or usually undertakes as the case may be to execute the work or which are otherwise under his control or management.

13. Remedies of employer against stranger

Where a workman has recovered compensation in respect of any injury caused under circumstances creating a legal liability of some person other than the person by whom the compensation was paid to pay damages in respect thereof the person by whom the compensation was paid and any person who has been called on to pay an indemnity under Section 12 shall be entitled to be indemnified by the person so liable to pay damages of aforesaid.

14. Insolvency of employer

Where any employer has entered into a contract with any insurers in respect of any liability under this Act to any workman then in the event of the employer becoming insolvent or making a compensation or scheme of arrangement with his creditors or if the employer is a company in the event of the company having commenced to be wound up the rights of the employer against the insurers as respects that liability shall notwithstanding anything in any law for the time being in force relating to insolvency or the winding up of companies be transferred to and vest in the workman and upon any such transfer the insurers shall have the same rights and remedies and be subject to the same liabilities as if they were the employer so however that the insurers shall not be under any greater liability to the workman than they would have been under the employer. If the liability of the insurers to the workman is less than the liability of the employer to the workman the workman may prove for the balance in the insolvency proceedings or liquidation. Where in any case such as is referred to in sub-section

(1) the contract of the employer with the insurers to void or voidable by reason of non-compliance on the part of the employer with any terms or conditions of the contract (other than a stipulation for the payment of premium) the provisions of that sub-section shall apply as if the contract were not void or voidable and the insurers shall be entitled to prove in the insolvency proceedings or liquidation for the amount paid to the workman :

Provided that the provisions of this sub-section shall not apply in any case in which the workman fails to give notice to the insurers of the happening of the accident and of any resulting disablement as soon as practicable after he becomes aware of the institution of the insolvency or liquidation proceedings.

There shall be deemed to be included among the debts which under Section 49 of the Presidency-towns Insolvency Act, 1909 (3 of 1909) or under Section 61 of the Provincial Insolvency Act, 1920 (5 of 1920) or under section 530 of the Companies Act, 1956 (1 of 1956) are in the distribution of the property of an insolvent or in the distribution of the assets of a company being wound up to be paid in priority to all other debts the amount due in respect of any compensation the liability where for accrued before the date of the order of adjudication of the insolvent or the date of the commencement of the winding up as the case may be and those Acts shall have effect accordingly. Where the compensation is a half-monthly payment the amount due in respect thereof shall for the purpose of this Section be taken to be the amount of the lump sum for which the half-monthly payment could if redeemable be redeemed if application was made for that purpose under section 7 and a certificate of the Commissioner as to the amount of such sum shall be conclusive proof thereof. The provisions of sub-Section (4) shall apply in the case of any amount for which an insurer is entitled to prove under sub-section (3) but otherwise those provisions shall not apply where the insolvent or the company being wound up has entered into such a contract with insurers as is referred to in sub-section (1). This Section shall not apply where a company is wound up voluntarily merely for the purposes of reconstruction or of amalgamation with another company.

14A. Compensation to be first charge on assets transferred by employer

Where an employer transfers his assets before any amount due in respect of any compensation the liability wherefor accrued before the date of the transfer has been paid such amount shall notwithstanding anything contained in any other law for the time being in force be a first charge on that part of the assets so transferred as consists of immovable property.

15. * * *

16. Returns as to compensation

The State Government may by notification in the Official Gazette direct that every person employing workmen or that any specified class of such persons shall send at such time and in such form and to such authority as may be specified in the notification a correct return specifying the number of injuries in respect of which compensation has been paid by the employer during the previous year and the amount of such compensation together with such other particulars as to the compensation as the State Government may direct.

17. Contracting out any contract or agreement

Whether made before or after the commencement of this Act whereby a workman relinquishes any right of compensation from the employer for personal injury arising out of or in the course of the employment shall be null and void in so far as it purports to remove or reduce the liability of any person to pay compensation under this Act.

18. Proof of age [Repealed by the Workmen's Compensation (Amendment) Act 1959, (8 of 1959)]

18A. Penalties

(1) Whoever—

(a) fails to maintain a notice-book which he is required to maintain under sub-section (3) of Section 10, or

(b) fails to send to the Commissioner a statement which he is required to send under sub-section (1) of Section 10A, or

(c) fails to send a report which he is required to send under Section 10B, or

(d) fails to make a return which he is required to make under Section 16 shall be punishable with fine which may extend to five thousand rupees.

(2) No prosecution under this Section shall be instituted except by or with the previous sanction of a Commissioner and no Court shall take cognizance of any offence under this Section unless complaint thereof is made within six months of the date on which the alleged commission of the offence came to the knowledge of the Commissioner.

19. Reference of Commissioners

If any question arises in any proceedings under this Act as to the liability of any person to pay compensation (including any question as to whether a person injured is or is not a workman) or as to the amount of duration of compensation (including any question as to the nature or extent of disablement) the question shall in default of agreement be settled by a Commissioner.

No civil court shall have jurisdiction to settle, decided or deal with any question which is by or under this Act required to be settled, decided or dealt with by a Commissioner or to enforce any liability incurred under this Act.

20. Appointment of Commissioners

(1) The State Government may by notification in the Official Gazette appoint any person to be a Commissioner for Workmen's Compensation for such area as may be specified in the notification.

(2) Where more than one Commissioner has been appointed

for any area the State Government may by general or special order regulate the distribution of business between them.

(3) Any Commissioner may for the purpose of deciding any matter referred to him for decision under this Act choose one or more persons possessing special knowledge of any matter relevant to the matter under inquiry to assist him in holding the inquiry.

(4) Every Commissioner shall be deemed to be a public servant within the meaning of the Indian Penal Code, 1860 (45 of 1860).

21. Venue of proceedings and transfer

(1) Where any matter under this Act is to be done by or before a Commissioner the same shall subject to the provisions of this Act and to any rules made hereunder be done by or before the Commissioner for the area in which—

(a) the accident took place which resulted in the injury; or

(b) the workman or in case of his death the dependant claiming the compensation ordinarily resides; or

(c) the employer has his registered office :

Provided that no matter shall be processed before or by a Commissioner other than the Commissioner having jurisdiction over the area in which the accident took place without his giving notice in the manner prescribed by the Central Government to the Commissioner having jurisdiction over the area and the State Government concerned:

Provided further that where the workman being the master of a ship or a seaman or the captain or a member of the crew of an aircraft or a workman in a motor vehicle or a company meets with the accident outside India any such matter may be done by or before a Commissioner for the area in which the owner or agent of the ship aircraft or motor vehicle resides or carries on business or the registered office of the company is situated as the case may be.

(1A) If a Commissioner other than the Commissioner with whom any money has been deposited under Section 8 proceeds with a matters under this Act the former may for the proper disposal of the matter call for transfer of any records or moneys remaining with the latter and on receipt of such a request he shall comply with the same.

(2) If a Commissioner is satisfied that any matter arising out of any proceedings pending before him can be more conveniently dealt with by any other Commissioner whether in the same State or not he may subject to rules made under this Act order such matter to be transferred to such other Commissioner either for report or for disposal and if he does so shall forthwith transmit to such other Commissioner all documents relevant for the decision of such matter and where the matter is transferred for disposal shall also transmit in the prescribed manner any money remaining in his hands or invested by him for the benefit of any party to the proceedings :

Provided that the Commissioner shall not where any party to the proceedings has appeared before him made any order of transfer relating to the distribution among dependants of a lump sum without giving such party an opportunity of being heard :

(3) The Commissioner to whom any matter is so transferred shall subject to rules made under this Act inquire there into and if the matter was transferred for disposal continue the proceedings as if they had originally commenced before him.

(4) On receipt of report from a Commissioner to whom any matter has been transferred for report under sub-section (2)

the Commissioner by whom it was referred shall decide the matter referred in conformity with such report.

(5) The State Government may transfer any matter from any Commissioner appointed by it to any other Commissioner appointed by it.

22. Form of application

(1) Where an accident occurs in respect of which liability to pay compensation under this Act arises a claim for such compensation may subject to the provisions of this Act be made before the Commissioner.

(1A) Subject to the provisions of sub-section (1) no application for the settlement of any matter of Commissioner other than an application by a dependant or dependants for compensation shall be made unless and until some question has arisen between the parties in connection therewith which they have been unable to settle by agreement.

(2) An application to a Commissioner may be made in such form and shall be accompanied by such fee if any as may be prescribed and shall contain in addition to any particulars which may be prescribed the following particulars namely:—

(a) A concise statement of the circumstances in which the application is made and the relief or order which the applicant claims;
(b) in the case of a claim for compensation against an employer the date of service of notice of the accident on the employer and if such notice has not been served or has not been served in due time the reason for such omission;
(c) the names and addresses of the parties; and
(d) except in the case of an application by dependants for compensation a concise statement of the matters on which agreement has and of those on which agreement has not been come to.

(3) If the applicant is illiterate or for any other reason is unable to furnish the required information in writing the application shall if the applicant so desires be prepared under the direction of the Commissioner.

22A. (1) Power of Commissioner to require further deposit in cases of fatal accident where any sum has been deposited by an employer as compensation payable in respect of a workman whose injury has resulted in death and in the opinion of the Commissioner such sum is insufficient the Commissioner may by notice in writing stating his reasons call upon the employer to show-cause why he should not make a further deposit within such time as may be stated in the notice.

(2) If the employer fails to show-cause to the satisfaction of the Commissioner may make an award determining the total amount payable and requiring the employer to deposit the deficiency.

23. Powers and procedure of Commissioners

The Commissioner shall have all the powers of a Civil Court under the Code of Civil Procedure, 1908 (5 of 1908) for the purpose of taking evidence on oath (which such Commissioner is hereby empowered to impose) and of enforcing the attendance of witnesses and compelling the production of documents and material objects and the Commissioner shall be deemed to be a Civil Court for all the purposes of Section 195 and of Chapter XXVI of the Code of Criminal Procedure 1973 (2 of 1974).

24. Appearance of parties

Any appearance application or act required to be made or done by any person before or to a Commissioner (other than an appearance of a party which is required for the purpose of his examination as a witness) may be made or done on behalf of such person by a legal practitioner or by an official of an Insurance company or a registered

Trade Union or by an Inspector appointed under sub-section (1) of Section 8 of the Factories Act, 1948 (63 of 1948) or under sub-section (1) of Section 5 of the Mines Act, 1952 (35 of 1952) or by any other officer specified by the State Government in this behalf authorised in writing by such person or with the permission of the Commissioner by any other person so authorised.

25. Method of recording evidence

The Commissioner shall make a brief memorandum of the substance of the evidence of every witness as the examination of the witness proceeds and such memorandum shall be written and signed by the Commissioner with his own hand and shall form part of the record :

> Provided that if the Commissioner is prevented from making such memorandum he shall record the reason of his inability to do so and shall cause such memorandum to be made in writing from his dictation and shall sign the same and such memorandum shall form part of the record: Provided further that the evidence of any medical witness shall be taking down as nearly as may be word for word.

26. Costs

All costs incidental to any proceedings before a Commissioner shall subject to rules made under this Act be in the discretion of the Commissioner.

27. Power of submit cases

A Commissioner may if he thinks fit submit any question of law for the decision of the High Court and if he does so shall decide the question in conformity with such decision.

28. Registration of agreements

(1) Where the amount of any lump sum payable as

compensation has been settled by agreement whether by way of redemption of a half-monthly payment or otherwise or where any compensation has been so settled as being payable to a woman or a person under a legal disability a memorandum thereof shall be sent by the employer to the Commissioner who shall on being satisfied as to its genuineness record the memorandum in a register in the prescribed manner :

Provided that—

(a) no such memorandum shall be recorded before seven days after communication by the Commissioner of notice to the parties concerned;

[Clause (b) omitted by Act 5 of 1929.]

(c) the Commissioner may at any time rectify the register;

(d) where it appears to the Commissioner that an agreement as to the payment of a lump sum whether by way of redemption of a half-monthly payment or otherwise or an agreement as to the amount of compensation payable to a woman or a person under a legal disability ought not to be registered by reason of the inadequacy of the sum or amount or by reason of the agreement having been obtained by fraud or undue influence or other improper means he may refuse to record the memorandum of the agreement and may make such order including an order as to any sum already paid under the agreement as he thinks just in the circumstances.

(2) An agreement for the payment of compensation which has been registered under sub-section (1) shall be enforceable under this Act notwithstanding anything contained in the Indian Contract Act 1872 (9 of 1872) or in any other law for the time being in force.

29. Failure to register agreement

Effect of failure to register agreement where a memorandum of any agreement the registration of which is required by Section 28 is not sent to the Commissioner as required by that Section the employer shall be liable to pay the full amount of compensation which he is liable to pay under the provisions of this Act and notwithstanding anything contained in the proviso to sub-section (1) of Section 4 shall not unless the Commissioner otherwise directs be entitled to deduct more than half of any amount paid to the workman by way of compensation whether under the agreement or otherwise.

30. Appeals

(1) An appeal shall lie to the High Court from the following orders of a Commissioner namely :—

(aa) an order as awarding as compensation a lump sum whether by way of redemption of a half-monthly payment or otherwise or disallowing a claim in full or in part for a lump sum;

(a) an order awarding interest or penalty under Section 4A;

(b) an order refusing to allow redemption of a half-monthly payment;

(c) an order providing for the distribution of compensation among the dependants of a deceased workman or disallowing any claim of a person alleging himself to be such dependant;

(d) an order allowing or disallowing any claim for the amount of an indemnity under the provisions of sub-section (2) of Section 12; or

(e) an order refusing to register a memorandum of agreement or registering the same or providing for the registration of the same subject to conditions :

Provided that no appeal shall lie against any order unless a substantial question of law is involved in the appeal and in the case of an order other than an order such as is referred to in clause (b) unless the amount in dispute in the appeal is not less than three hundred rupees :

Provided further that no appeal shall lie in any case in which the parties have agreed to abide by the decision of the Commissioner or in which the order of the Commissioner gives effect to an agreement come to by the parties :

Provided further that no appeal by an employer under clause (a) shall lie unless the memorandum of appeal is accompanied by a certificate by the Commissioner to the effect that the appellant has deposited with him the amount payable under the order appealed against.

The period of limitation for an appeal under this Section shall be sixty days.

(2) The provisions of Section 5 of the Limitation Act, 1963 (36 of 1963) shall be applicable to appeals under this Section.

30A. Withholding of certain payments pending decision of appeal

Where an employer makes an appeal under clause (a) of sub-section (1) of Section 30 the Commissioner may and if so directed by the High Court shall pending the decision of the appeal withhold payment of any sum in deposit with him.

31. Recovery

The Commissioner may recover as an arrear of land revenue any amount payable by any person under this Act whether under an agreement for the payment of compensation or otherwise and the Commissioner shall be deemed to be a public officer within the meaning of Section 5 of the Revenue Recovery Act, 1890 (1 of 1890).

SCHEDULE I [Sections 2(1) and (4)]

Part I

List of Injuries Deemed to Result in Permanent Total Disablement

S.No. Description of injury Percentage of loss of earning capacity :

1. Loss of both hands or amputation at higher sites 100
2. Loss of a hand and a foot 100
3. Double amputation through leg or thigh, or amputation through leg or thigh on one side and loss of other foot 100
4. Loss of sight to such an extent as to render the claimant unable to perform any work for which eye-sight is essential 100
5. Very severe facial disfigurement 100
6. Absolute deafness 100

Part II

List of injuries Deemed to Result in Permanent Partial Disablement

Amputation cases-upper limbs (either arm) :

1. Amputation through shoulder joint 90
2. Amputation below shoulder with stump less than 20.32 cms from tip of acromion 80
3. Amputation from 20.32 cms from tip of acromion to less than 11.43 cms below tip of olecranon 70
4. Loss of a hand or of the thumb and four fingers of one hand or amputation from 11.43 cms below tip of olecranon 60
5. Loss of thumb 30
6. Loss of thumb and its metacarpal bone 40
7. Loss of four fingers of one hand 50
8. Loss of three fingers of one hand 30
9. Loss of two fingers of one hand 20
10. Loss of terminal phalanx of thumb 20

Amputation cases-lower limbs

11. Amputation of both feet resulting in end bearing stumps 90
12. Amputation through both feet proximal to the metatarsophalangeal joint 80
13. Loss of all toes of both feet through the metatarso-phalngeal joint 40
14. Loss of all toes of both feet proximal inter-phalangeal joint 30
15. Loss of all toes of both feet distal to the proximal inter-phalangeal joint 20
16. Amputation at hip 90
17. Amputation below hip with stump not exceeding 12.70 cms in length measured from tip of great trochanter 80
18. Amputation below hip with stump exceeding 12.70 cms in length measured from tip of great trochanter but not beyond middle thigh 70
19. Amputation below middle thigh to 8.89 cms below knee 60
20. Amputation below knee with stump exceeding 8.89 cms but not exceeding 12.70 cms 50
21. Amputation below knee with stump exceeding 12.70 cms 50
22. Amputation of one foot resulting in end bearing stump 50
23. Amputation through one foot proximal to the metatarso-phalangeal joint 50
24. Loss of all toes one foot through the metatarso-phalangeal joint 20

Other Injuries

25. Loss of one eye, without complication, the other being normal 40
26. Loss of vision of one eye, without complications or disfigurement of eye-ball, the other being normal 30

26 A. Loss of partial vision of one eye 10

Loss of A. Fingers of right or left hand

Index Finger

27. Whole 14
28. Two phalanges 11
29. One phalanx 9
30. Guillotine amputation of tip without loss of bone 5

Middle Finger

31. Whole 12
32. Two phalanges 9
33. One phalanx 7
34. Guillotine amputation of tip without loss of bone 4

Ring or Little Finger

35. Whole 7
36. Two phalanges 6
37. One phalanx 5
38. Gulliotine amputation of tip without loss of bone 2
38. B. Toes of right or left foot

Great Toe

39. Through metatarso-phalanges joint 14
40. Part, with some loss of bone 3

Any other Toe

41. Through metatarso-phalangeal joint 3
42. Part, with some loss of bone 1

Two Toes of One Foot, Excluding Great Toe

43. Through metatarso-phalangeal joint 5
44. Part, with some loss of bone 1

Three Toes of one Foot, Excluding Great Toe

45. Through metatarso-phalangeal joint 6
46. Part, with some loss of bone 3

Four Toes of one Foot, Excluding Great Toe

47. Through metatarso-phalangeal joint 9
48. Part with some loss of bone 3

Note: Complete and permanent loss of the use of any limb or member referred to in the Schedule shall be deemed to be the equivalent of the loss of that limb or member.

SCHEDULE II [Section 2(1)(n)]

List of Persons who Subject to the provisions of Section 2(1)(n) are included in the Definition of Workmen

The following persons are workmen within the meaning of Section 2(1)(n) and subject to the provisions of that Section that is to say any person who is—

1. employed otherwise than in a clerical capacity or on a railway in connection with the operation repair or maintenance of a lift or a vehicle propelled by steam or other mechanical power or by electricity or in connection with the loading or unloading of any such vehicle; or
2. employed otherwise than in clerical capacity in any premises wherein or within the precincts whereof a

manufacturing process as defined in clause (k) of Section 2 of the Factories Act, 1948 (63 of 1948) is being carried on or in any kind of work whatsoever incident to or connected with any such manufacturing process or with the article made whether or not employment in any such work is within such premises or precincts and steam water or other mechanical power or electrical power is used; or

3. employed for the purpose of making altering repairing ornamenting finishing or otherwise adapting for use transport or sale any article or part of an article in any premises wherein or within the precincts whereof twenty or more person are so employed.

   Explanation : For the purposes of this clause persons employed outside such premises or precincts but in any work incidental to or connected with the work relating to making altering repairing ornamenting finishing or otherwise adapting for use transport or sale of any article or part of an article shall be deemed to be employed within such premises or precincts; or
4. employed in the manufacture or handling of explosives in connection with the employer's trade or business; or
5. employed in any mine as defined in clause (j) of Section 2 of the Mines Act, 1952 (35 of 1952) in any mining operation or in any kind of work other than clerical work incidental to or connected with any mining operation or with the mineral obtained or in any kind or work whatsoever below ground; or
6. employed as the master or as a seaman of—

   (a) any ship which is propelled wholly or in part by steam or other mechanical power of by electricity or which is towed or intended to be towed by a ship so propelled; or

   (b) any ship not included in sub-clause (a) of twenty-five tonnes net tonnage or over; or

   (c) any sea-going ship not included in sub-clause (a) or

sub-clause (b) provided with sufficient area for navigation under sails alone; or

7. Employed for the purpose of—

(a) loading unloading fuelling constructing repairing demolishing cleaning or painting any ship of which he is not the master or a member of the crew or handling or transport within the limits of any post subject to the Indian Ports Act, 1908 (15 of 1908) or the Major Port Trusts Act, 1963 (18 of 1963) of goods which have been discharged from or are to be loaded into any vessel; or
(b) warping a ship through the lock; or
(c) mooring and unmooring ships at harbour wall berths or in pier; or
(d) removing or replacing dry dock caissons when vessels are entering or leaving dry docks; or
(e) the docking or undocking of any vessel during an emergency; or
(f) preparing splicing chir springs and check wires painting depth marks on locksides removing or replacing fenders whenever necessary landing of gangways maintaining lifebuoys up to standard or any other maintenance work of a like nature; or
(g) any work on jolly boats for bringing a ship's line to the wharf; or

8. Employed in the construction maintenance repair or demolition of —

(a) any building which is designed to be or is or has been more than one storey in height above the ground or twelve feet or more from the ground level to the apex of the roof, or
(b) any dam or embankment which is twelve feet or more in height from its lowest to its highest point; or

(c) any road bridge tunnel or canal; or

(d) any wharf quay sea wall or other marine work including any moorings of ships; or

9. employed in setting up maintaining repairing or taking down any telegraph or telephone line or post or any overhead electric line or cable or standard or fittings and fixtures for the same; or

10 employed otherwise than in a clerical capacity in the construction working repair or demolition of any aerial ropeway canal pipeline or sewer; or

11. employed in the service of any fire brigade; or

12. employed upon a railway as defined in clause (31) of Section 2 and sub-section (1) of Section 197 of the Indian Railway Act, 1989 (24 of 1989) either directly or through a sub-contractor by a person fulfilling a contract with the railway administration; or

13. employed as an inspector mail guard sorter or van peon in the Railway Mail Service or as a telegraphist or as a postal or railway signaller or employed in any occupation ordinarily involving outdoor work in the Indian Posts and Telegraphs Department; or

14. employed otherwise than in a clerical capacity in connection with operations for winning natural petroleum or natural gas; or

15. employed in any occupation involving blasting operations; or

16. employed in the making of any excavaction in which on any one day of the preceding twelve months more than twenty-five persons have been employed or explosives have been used or whose depth from its highest to its lowest point exceeds twelve feet; or

17. employed in the operation of any ferry boat capable of carrying more than ten person; or

18. employed otherwise than in a clerical capacity on any estate which is maintained for the purpose of growing cardamom cinchona coffee rubber or tea and on which on any one

day in the preceding twelve months twenty-five or more persons have been so employed; or

19. employed otherwise than in a clerical capacity in the generating transforming transmitting or distribution of electrical energy or in generation or supply of gas; or
20. employed in a lighthouse as defined in clause (d) of Section 2 of the Indian Lighthouse Act 1927 (17 of 1927); or
21. employed in producing cinematograph pictures intended for public exhibition or in exhibiting such pictures; or
22. employed in the training keeping or working of elephants or wild animals; or
23. employed in the tapping of palm trees or the felling or logging of trees or the transport of timber by inland waters or the control or extinguishing or forests fires; or
24. employed in operations for the catching or hunting of elephants or other wild animals; or
25. employed as a diver; or
26. employed in the handling or transport of goods in or within the precincts of—
    (a) any warehouse or other place in which goods are stored and in which on any one day of the preceding twelve months ten or more persons have been so employed; or
    (b) any market in which on any one day of the preceding twelve months fifty or more persons have been so employed; or
27. employed in any occupation involving the handling and manipulation of radium or X-ray apparatus or contract with radioactive substances; or
28. employed in or in connection with the construction erection dismantling operation or maintenance of an aircraft as defined in Section 2 of the Indian Aircraft Act, 1934 (22 of 1934); or
29. employed in horticultural operations forestry bee keeping or framing by tractors or other contrivances driven by steam or other mechanical power or by electricity; or

30. employed otherwise than in a clerical capacity in the construction working repair or maintenance of a tube well; or
31. employed in the maintenance repair or renewal of electric fittings in any building; or
32. employed in a circus;
33. employed as watchman in any factory or establishment; or
34. employed in any operation in the sea for catching fish;
35. employed in any employment which requires handling of snakes for the purpose of extraction of venom or for the purpose of looking after snakes or handling any other poisonous animal or insects; or
36. employed in handling animals like horses mules and bulls;
37. employed for the purpose of loading or unloading any mechanically propelled vehicle or in the handling or transport of goods which have been loaded in such vehicles;
38. employed in cleaning of sewer lines or septic tanks within the limits of a local authority;
39. employed on surveys and investigation exploration or garage or discharge observation of rivers including drilling operations hydrological observations and flood forecasting activities groundwater surveys and exploration;
40. employed in cleaning of jungles or reclaiming land or ponds in which on any one day of the preceding twelve months more than twenty-five persons have been employed;
41. employed in cultivation of land or rearing and maintenance of livestock or forest operations or fishing in which on any one day of the preceding twelve months more than twenty-five persons have been employed;
42. employed in installation maintenance or repair of pumping equipment used for lifting of water from wells tube wells ponds lakes streams and the like;
43. employed in the construction boring or deepening of an open well bore well bore-cum-dug well filter point and the like;

44. employed in spraying and dusting of insecticides or pesticides in agricultural operations or plantations; or
45. employed in mechanised harvesting and threshing operations;
46. employed in working or repair or maintenance of bulldozers tractors power tillers and the like;
47. employed as artists for drawing pictures on advertisement boards at a height of 3.66 metres or more from the ground level;
48. employed in any newspaper establishment as defined in the Working Journalists and Other Newspaper Employees (Conditions of Services) and Miscellaneous Provisions Act, 1955 (45 of 1955) and engaged in outdoor work.

    Explanation: In this Schedule the preceding twelve months relates in any particular case to the twelve months ending with the day on which the accident in such case occurred.

SCHEDULE III [Section 3]

List of Occupational Diseases

1. Infectious and parasitic diseases contracted in an occupation where there is a particular risk of contaminaion :
    (a) All work involving exposure to health or laboratory work;
    (b) All work involving exposure to veterinary work;
    (c) Work relating to handling animals, animal carcasses or merchandise which may have been contaminated by animals or animal carcasses;
    (d) Other work carrying a particular risk of contamination.

2. Disease caused by work in compressed air. All work involving exposure to the risk concerned.
3. Diseases caused by lead or its toxic compounds. All work involving exposure to the risk concerned.
4. Poisoning by nitrous fumes. All work involving exposure to the risk concerned.

5. Poisoning by organophosphorus compounds. All work involving exposure to the risk concerned.

Part B

1. Diseases caused by phosphorus or its toxic compounds. All work involving exposure to the risk concerned.
2. Diseases caused by mercury or its toxic compounds. All work involving exposure to the risk concerned.
3. Diseases caused by benzene or its toxic homologues. All work involving exposure to the risk concerned.
4. Diseases caused by nitro and amino toxic derivatives of benzene or its homologous. All work involving exposure to the risk concerned.

BIBLIOGRAPHY

Agarwal, Bina, *A Field of One's Own: Gender and Land Rights in South Asia,* Cambridge University Press, Cambridge, 1994.

Batliwala, Srilata, *Fields of Rice-Health Hazards for Women and Unborn Children,* In Manushi, No. 46, Bangalore, 1983.

GOI, *Report of the Study Group on Women and Child Labour,* National Commission on Labour, Ministry of Labour, Govt. of India, New Delhi, 2002.

GOI, *Report of the Taskforce on Employment*, Planning Commission, Govt. of India, New Delhi, 2001.

GOI, *Shramshakti* Report of the National Commission on self-employed women and women in informal sector, Govt. of India, New Delhi, 1988.

IFAD, *Gender Strengthen Programme for Eastern and Southern Africa*, International Fund for Agriculture Development, 2000 (www.ifad.org).

ILO, *Encyclopaedia of Occupational Health and Safety,* 3rd Rev. Ed., Vol. I. AK, International Labour Office, Geneva, 1983.

Itano, Nicole. *Despite Promises Zimbabwean Women not Given Land,* In Women's E News, 2002 (www.womenwagingpeace.net).

Jain, P.C., Jain, S. and Bhatnagar, S. *Scheduled Caste Women*, Rawat Publications, New Delhi, 1997.

Mahapatra, S. *Women Participation in Labour Force,* Rajat Publications, New Delhi, 2002.

Meena, N.L. *'National Policy and Programmes for Women in India'* In *Papers and Proceedings of the Regional Conference on Gender Issues in Agriculture,* Manila, December, 5-6, 1990, Asian Development Bank and United Nations Development Fund for Women, 1991.

Ministry of Labour, *Employment Review* (Jan.-March), New Delhi, 1999.

Nagaraj, K. *Female Workers in Rural Tamil Nadu: A Preliminary Study,* Asian Development Programme, International Labour Organisation, New Delhi. 1988.

NSSO—50th Round, Report No. 10, *Employment and Unemployment*, National Sample Survey Organisation,

Government of India, New Delhi, 1994.

NSSO—53rd Round, Report No. 442, *Household Consumer Expenditure and Employment Situation in India,* National Sample Survey Organisation, Government of India, 1997.

NSSO—55th Round, Report No. 455, *Informal Non-Agricultural Enterprises,* National Sample Survey Organisation, Government of India, New Delhi, 2000.

Punia, R.K.*Women in Agriculture. Education, Training and Development,* Vol. 2, Northern Book Centre, New Delhi, 1992.

Rai, C. P., *Working Women in India,* In *Working Women and Children Series,* Laxmi Shiksha Sansthan, Lucknow, Anmol Publications Pvt. Limited, New Delhi, 2002.

Rogers, D. and Vandeman, A. *Women Farm Landlords in the United States,* Agricultural Information Bulletin No. 681, USDA, Washington, DC, 1993.

Sharma, Alakh N. and Singh, Seema, *Women and Work Changing Scenario in India,* Indian Society of Labour Economics, Patna, 1993.

Swaminathan, M.S. *Indian Agriculture: Looking Back and Forward,* In *Yojana,* ISSN-0971-8400, New Delhi, 1997.

Swaminathan, Mina. *WHO CARES? A study of child care facilities for low income women in India,* Centre for Women's Development Studies, New Delhi, 1985.

UNDP, *Human Development Report,* United Nations Development Programme, Oxford University Press, New York, 1997.

Unni, J. *Women Workers in Agriculture: Some Recent Trends,* In *Gender and Employment in India*, Papola, TS and Alakh N. Sharma (Eds.), Vikas Publishing House, New Delhi, 1999

USDA, *Status Report on Minority and Women Farmers in the US in Agricultural Outlook* United States, Department of Agriculture, Economic Research Service, May, 1998.

USDA, *Women in Agricultural Development* (Tape # 503), United States, Department of Agriculture, 2000.

Venkateswaran, S. *Living on the Edge: Women, Environment and Development,* Friedrich Ebert Stiftung, New Delhi, 1992.

Verma, B. *Exploitation of Women Labour in India Employment Pattern and Wage Discrimination,* Deep and Deep Publications, New Delhi, 1993.

World Bank, *A World Bank Country Report: Gender and Poverty in India,* World Bank, Washington DC, 1991.

INDEX